NIGERIA'S LEADERSHIP ROLE IN AFRICA

NIGERIA'S LEADERSHIP ROLE IN AFRICA

Dr Joseph Wayas

© Joseph Wayas 1979

First published 1979 by
THE MACMILLAN PRESS LTD
London and Basingstoke
Associated companies in Delhi
Dublin Hong Kong Johannesburg Lagos
Melbourne New York Singapore Tokyo

Printed in Great Britain by
Billing & Sons Limited
Guildford, London and Worcester

British Library Cataloguing in Publication Data

Wayas, Joseph
  Nigeria's leadership role in Africa
  1. Nigeria – Foreign relations   2. Africa
  – Foreign relations
  I. Title
  301.5′92   DT515.62

  ISBN 0-333-26295-6
  ISBN 0-333-27037-1 Pbk

For my wife Mary and my children Donna, Joey,
Godwin and Florence

Contents

1 Introduction

Any reasonable discussion of African affairs or problems today must necessarily begin by dealing with two fashionable but mutually contradicting half-truths or misconceptions. Both half-truths derive from attempts to answer one basic question: Why is Africa so far behind all other continents and sub-continents in terms of economic development? One group of 'analysts' have generally answered this question by insisting, quite correctly, I think, that it is because of European colonialism. The argument of this group generally goes like this: the Europeans came into Africa with a bible and a gun under the guise of bringing Christian civilisation. In the process they killed and enslaved millions of Africans, and then stole their lands and natural resources. Unfortunately, these statements are historically true. But the argument never ends there. Its exponents insist, with amusing ruefulness perhaps, that the European presence destroyed not only the African's culture and traditional institutions, but even his mental capacity to cope with the present. Thus, all the past and present failures and shortcomings of African governments and even of individual citizens, are, without any discrimination what-soever, blamed on colonialism and the white man. Even such is the one-sided vehemence with which this view is promulgated that today many Africans are not in the least bashful in tracing the 'origin' of the chronic corruption in African countries to some vague point in the colonial era.

There is, however, an opposing view to this, though equally extreme. It is only just emerging and it is more fashionable among intellectuals. In the cunning way of a university professor, these intellectuals, while admitting the bruising effect of colonialism, nonetheless argue that the phenomenon took place so long ago that we should now forget it and instead concentrate on the present and the future. This they call the reality of the present. And again the argument sounds reasonable. But what it actually does is to create a dichotomy between the past and the present in such a way that the past is considered irrelevant to solving the problems of the present. These intellectuals are thus suspicious—even contemptuous— of those leaders who formulate policies that openly take cognisance of the colonial past; or even worse, who attribute, in any way or form, their economic problems to external forces.

But it should be noted from the outset that it would require a deadening of the mind to forget the record of European colonialism in Africa or, for that matter, to sweep it aside. The effects of colonialism have been both subtle and glaring. Walter Rodney, in his popular book *How Europe Under-developed Africa* (Dar-es-Salaam: Tanzania Publishing House, 1972) has dealt at great length with the issue of how European administrations and trading companies deliberately and systematically worked to stagnate Africa's economic growth. He stresses the point that bringing the continent into the world economy or, more correctly, the European economic system, while it obviously had its advantages, was perhaps the beginning of Africa's economic problems. It was the beginning of the still-growing disequilibrium between European and African economic development, because the latter was forced into the market system at a competitive disadvantage. Possessing no advanced technological know-how (say, to build ships and to cross the oceans to European markets), Africa was in no position to compete with European entrepreneurs. This resulted in a one-way trade. Europeans exploited Africa's mineral and other natural resources, which they shipped to European factories and markets without paying a just price for them, and in return they dumped on Africa cheap and useless goods. The net effect of this, of course, was that Africa became a dependent economy, serving European markets and tastes, and thus externally controlled and regulated from European centres. These problems were not solved by European physical exit from Africa at the time of independence. They still confront African countries, even on an increasing scale. Samir Amin also deals with these problems in his book *Neo-colonialism in West Africa* (New York: Monthly Review Press, 1973), in which he examines the economic dependence on France of former French colonies. Amin sees it as a problem of 'outward-directed' growth, that is growth based on external demand and external financing. Pointedly he says:

'The speeding up of colonial exploitation after the Second World War accentuated the structural characteristics of under-development in this part of Africa. It transformed the area from the stage of being a primitive 'reserve', virtually outside the world market, into that of a true under-developed economy: dominated by and integrated into the world market, and with a 'dualistic' appearance; characterized by an increasing inequality in the distribution of growth between the various sectors and of the *per capita* product. The outward-directed character became more marked and there was an increasing dependence on the centre, which stimulated and maintained this growth from the outside.

(op. cit., p. xiv)

Again, talking about the Senegal groundnut economy, Amin says:

. . . These choices were not made because the colonial State was not interested in the development of the colony, but in its usefulness for home needs: to provide very cheap oil for French consumers by underpaying the African peasants for their work. The mistake was to continue the concentration on groundnuts after independence.

(op. cit., p. xv)

The outward-directedness, or the one-way nature of European

trade with Africa, is perhaps more forcefully summarised by the following statements by two (British and French) colonials:

> British trade is a magnificent superstructure of American commerce and naval power on an African foundation (Malachi Posttethwayt).
>
> If you were to lose each year more than 200 million livres that you now get from your colonies; if you had not the exclusive trade with your colonies to feed your manufactures, to maintain your navy, to keep your agriculture going, to repay for your imports, to provide for your luxury needs, to advantageously balance your trade with Europe and Asia, then I say it clearly, the kingdom would be irretrievably lost. (Bishop Maury of France)
>
> (Walter Rodney, op. cit., p. 84)

Both Samir Amin and Walter Rodney also raise another issue that is as significant as that of the outward-directedness of Africa's economic growth, if not more so. It is the balkanisation of the continent into a multiplicity of tiny and mostly unviable States. In other words, the disintegrating factor. Rodney has this to say:

> It has now become common knowledge that one of the principal reasons why genuine industrialization cannot easily be realised in Africa today is that the market for manufactured goods in any single African country is too small, and there is no integration of the markets across large areas of Africa. The kind of relationship which Africa has had with Europe from the beginning has worked in a direction opposite to integration of local economies.
>
> (op. cit., p. 119)

Amin makes a case of former French Colonies, of which the individual economies are so precarious that France has to pay part of their budgets to discourage them from federating with one another. He also makes a specific case with Gambia:

The Gambia receives a large amount of public aid from abroad, about 1 million Gambian pounds a year, which covers the whole of State expenditure on capital goods, or about 8 per cent of the GDP . . . This contribution is much greater in relative terms than that which Great Britain allows the other African Member States of the Commonwealth, and brings the level of 'aid' received by the Gambia to that of Senegal. Here again, this 'aid' has the effect of maintaining a non-viable State and perpetuating the balkanization of Africa. Without it, it is possible that the Gambia would have been forced to seek closer links with Senegal, or even to accept economic union.

(op. cit., p. 31)

Thus it is correct to say, as many observers have noted, that the problem was not, and has not been, the fact that Africa was brought into the world market system, but rather the manner in which it was introduced. Having an economic relationship with Europe was not in itself a bad idea; what was bad was the nature of the relationship. The fight which African countries are waging today is therefore a fight, not to eliminate the relationship, but to change it so that Africa can move away from her present situation of economic dependence and subordination.

Now, having said all this, does it mean that all present economic and political problems of the continent are to be traced to colonialism or to Europe? And how do we reconcile the two mutually contradicting viewpoints we began with?

Here we may have to seek some answer from what Dr Kwame Nkrumah said when he was confronted with the same problem:

All available evidence from the history of Africa, up to the eve of the European colonization, shows that African society was neither classless nor devoid of a social hierarchy. Feudalism existed in some parts of Africa before Colonization; and feudalism involves a deep and exploitative social stratification, founded on the ownership of land. It must also be noted that slavery existed in Africa before European colonization, although the earlier European contact gave slavery in Africa some of its most vicious characteristics. The truth remains, however, that before colonization, which became widespread in Africa only in the nineteenth century, Africans were prepared to sell, often for no more than thirty pieces of silver, fellow tribesmen and even members of the same 'extended' family and clan. Colonialism deserves to be blamed for many evils in Africa, but surely it was not preceded by an African Golden Age or paradise.

(Kwame Nkrumah, *The Struggle Continues*, London: Panaf Books, 1973, pp. 79–80)

A number of these evils can be specifically indicated. But here I am not concerned with the mental damage caused by colonialism, nor with the so-called destruction of our culture. Obviously, when two cultures clash, no one can be said to survive in tact, not even the dominant one. Moreover, as has been indicated many times by many thoughtful men, the coming together of any two cultures never, except in very few cases, results in retrogression for either, but rather a forward movement for both. In this regard, African culture has been no exception. Whilst there are certain values in traditional, i.e. pre-colonial, African societies, which we would be glad to recapture, it is equally true that there are certain facets of those pre-colonial societies which, as Nkrumah's statement suggests, we would be glad never to see resurrected. But, since the subject of this book is neither aesthetics nor philosophy, it is irrelevant to continue in this direction. What is important, however, is that the brief discussion reminds us of certain values of pre-colonial African society—for instance, humaneness—which have been seen by many African leaders today as relevant to formulating economic and political policies and are thus also relevant to the issue of the welfare of Africans. And this, in the last analysis, is central to the issues I intend to raise in this book.

But from here we can now proceed to examine, in a general way some of the approaches—call them ideological approaches—which many African political leaders have advocated and followed in solving the problems so far enumerated. Not only the problems of economic and political freedom from the domination of the industrialised West and the Soviet Union, but also of liberating Africans still languishing under the oppression of white, racist minority régimes in Southern Africa. They are the problems of achieving true economic and political independence and, equally, of putting one final end to the resurgence of colonialism (neo-colonialism). How to achieve these objectives has, to date, presented African leaders with the greatest dilemmas.

From the time of independence from direct colonial rule, many leaders have advocated and, in some cases adopted, various approaches and stances. Leaders like Kwame Nkrumah of Ghana, Modibo Keita of Mali and Sekou Toure of Guinea, and a few others of the early leaders, have advocated scientific socialism as the best path of development and of achieving real independence. Nkrumah, especially, urged this path of development within the framework of an African Continental Union Government. For him, the unification of all Africa into one colossus similar to the United States, the Soviet Union or China, would not only create a more united front and thus a more dynamic force against white oppression in those parts of the continent where white minority and racist régimes still exist, but would also result in the realisation of a larger and therefore more viable market for the continent's agricultural and industrial products. Moreover, such a union, acting with one voice and formulating a united policy of development, would be better able to exercise control over the continent's abundant natural resources and thus prevent exploitation. Obviously, the ideas and formulae of these leaders were never as simple and pert as I have expressed them here. Indeed, some of these concepts were couched in difficult and bombastic language, and these leaders invariably employed high-handedness in pursuit of them. And it is true that the vigour with which they tried to impress their ideas on the continent scared a lot of thoughtful leaders into outright rejection and, indeed, opposition to them. Thus the true essence of these ideas was never contemplated. These leaders were vilified and considered 'heretics', 'Communists' and 'power-grabbing maniacs', whose only true ambition was the acquisition of power. Dr Nkrumah, the most hated, feared, and most violently abused and maligned of these 'Communists', was pointedly branded a dictator who saw in the creation of a Continental Union Government the opportunity to become President of Africa. But it would be correct to say that the worst crime that Nkrumah and other like-minded leaders committed was of being visionary. And ever since taking the reins of power since independence only the dread of being overthrown has surpassed the dread that most African leaders have of having around them men with foresight, who see far ahead of the immediate present.

Nkrumah and Keita were overthrown on charges of mismanaging their countries' economies. But from disclosures in the United States we have since learned that the overthrow of these men had nothing to do with mismanagement of economies, but rather was externally inspired by foreign interests; and that these foreign interests were in turn compelled to move against these men, especially Nkrumah, because of a fear of their success at extricating their economies from foreign control. This appraisal is obliquely indicated by Roger Genoud in his book, *Nationalism and Economic Development in Ghana* (Montreal: Centre for Developing Area Studies, McGill University; New York: Praeger, 1969) Nkrumah and Keita are dead and gone and, as is often the case, only now do we begin to realise how true their voices were. What is significant here, however, is the new awareness that African success in economic development and liberation of her territories will never be easy, smooth or peaceful.

Of course, other thoughtful African leaders have espoused

brilliant concepts and have advocated development paths that take into consideration the peculiar circumstances of their own country, which they see as the best way of overcoming foreign political, economic and cultural oppression. Here, Julius Nyerere's African Socialism stands out. Nyerere's theory of development is buttressed on the ethic of self-reliance as a way of freeing the country from the dependency psychosis which Western foreign aid and its concomitant external control of the economy often entails. But Nyerere's success, while commended, is naturally limited. This is not because of a lack of personal commitment to follow his own stated ideas, nor even because of their incorrectness; but, rather, because Tanzania is pitifully poor in natural resources.

Since the espousal of set theories and ideas by Nkrumah, Keita and Nyerere, other African leaders have promulgated with great fanfares other variants of socialism. There are Kenneth Kaunda's *Humanism*, Jomo Kenyatta's *African Socialism*, Leopold Sanghor's *Democratic Socialism*, which is almost entirely based on linkage with the decadent socialism of the so-called West European democrats. Then there are Obote's *Common Man's Charter* and Seretse Khama's *Kagisano*. Today, variants of 'socialism' abound in the continent. While some of these philosophical enunciations are no doubt made with conviction and earnestness, it is equally true to say that most are mainly for public consumption. Because they are so facile and shallow, they are easily converted by party stalwarts into sentimental slogans that, rather than explain planned programmes of development and political action, are used in making cults of the presidents and prime ministers or with whatever other titles the leaders are endowed. Martin Minogue, in his introduction to *African Aims and Attitudes* (ed. with Judith Molloy, London: Cambridge University Press, 1974), has noted some of the characteristics of these ideologies:

A second, slightly baffling, characteristic of African Socialism is the co-existence of significant elements of vagueness and precision. The controlling ideology is only vaguely defined; the precision comes in the concrete planning mechanisms which purport to translate the ideology into practice. The vagueness serves a useful purpose to the politician: it provides symbols around which his supporters may cluster, without the rigidity which might cause embarrassing doctrinal divisions. And if, as so often occurs, concrete plans fail to realize their intentions, the ideology may conveniently be reinterpreted to cover up the failure, or at best, to explain it away. It is this syndrome which, perhaps, explains the recurrence in African socialist ideology of juxtaposed elements of pragmatism and utopianism.

Thus, in most cases, these philosophies or ideologies, full of generous sentiments and of high-minded purpose in their strong expression of desire and commitment to work to rid their countries and other parts of Africa of foreign domination and oppression, are often contrary to policies which these very leaders actually pursue. A few examples of this will suffice. Long ago, in December 1962, at The Dakar Colloqium on African Socialism (published in *Africa Report*, VIII, May 1963, and quoted in Minogue and Molloy, op. cit., pp. 167–73), Senghor sought to explain African socialism with such fervour:

> It is clear that our Socialism can no longer be exactly like that of Marx and Engels which was elaborated about a hundred years ago according to the scientific methods and circumstances of the nineteenth century and of Western Europe . . . Our African Socialism, then, will be elaborated not in the dependence but in the autonomy of our thought, and it will choose the most scientific, up-to-date, and, above all, the most efficient methods and institutions and techniques of the Western World and elsewhere. But in the final analysis, they will be efficient only if adapted to the African situations as it is, above all to our geography, history, culture and psychology.

The reader should judge the above only in the light of the fact that after so many years of persistent effort, Senghor was finally admitted in 1977 as a member of the West European Socialists.

We can take another example from Kenyatta, who defined his Kenyan brand of African Socialism in the following glowing terms:

In the phrase 'African Socialism', the word 'African' is not introduced to describe a continent to which a foreign ideology is to be transplanted. It is meant to convey the African roots of a system that is itself African in its characteristics. African Socialism is a term describing an African political and economic system that is positively African, not being imported from any country or being a blueprint of any foreign ideology but capable of incorporating useful and compatible techniques from whatever source. The principal conditions the system must satisfy are:

(i) it must draw on the best African traditions;

(ii) it must be adaptable to new rapidly changing circumstances; and

(iii) it must not rest for its success on a satellite relationship with any other country or group of countries.

There are two African traditions which form an essential basis for African Socialism – political democracy and mutual Social responsibility. Political democracy implies that each member of society is equal in his political rights and that no individual or group will be permitted to exert undue influence on the policies of the State. The State, therefore, can never become the tool of special interests, catering to the desires of a minority at the expense of the needs of the majority. The State will represent all of the people and will do so impartially and without prejudice.

(*African Socialism and its Application to Planning in Kenya*. Kenya Government Sessional Paper no. 10, 1965, Nairobi, 1965.)

How well Kenyatta has put the above into practice is another question. But many people will agree that Oginga Odinga's appraisal of its success as of 1966 is not too far off from the truth, and it may even be pertinent to the way most other African leaders have put their ideologies into effect:

> In the mouths of the Government and KANU leaders, 'African Socialism' has become a meaningless phrase. What they call 'African Socialism' is neither African nor Socialism. It is a cloak for the practice of total capitalism. To describe the policies of the present Government as 'African Socialism' is an insult to the intelligence of the people. The deception is obvious but the leaders of the Government and of KANU do not have the courage to admit that they are fully committed to the Western ideology of capitalism.
> (quoted in Minogue and Molloy, op. cit., see pp. 129–57)

But the sadness here, of course, is not that some of these ideologies are deficient. Rather, it is that these leaders, while professing to work towards the same goals for the benefit of their own people and of the continent, are invariably working at cross-purposes with one another with the result that, at least from a continental perspective, the good efforts of one are weakened, if not negated, by the docile and betraying stance of the other.

It is not surprising, then, that since the immediate period after independence, nearly all African leaders have believed they could solve the problems of their individual countries and those of the continent at large by enthusiastically relying on international forums such as the United Nations and its associated agencies, where they have often hoped to appeal to the conscience of the world. And this in spite of the fact that they should have realised right from the start that the industrialised countries, especially the Western countries who dominate and control the affairs of the United Nations and its international agencies, are the very ones who exploit the continent and her peoples; that these Western countries are the very ones that have helped maintain apartheid in South Africa, Zimbabwe and Namibia and Portuguese fascism in Angola, Mozambique and Guinea-Bissau; in short that these same countries are those against which the fight for freedom in Southern Africa is aimed. Perhaps, even more fundamentally, these African leaders should have realised all along that the problems of economic development are not solved through appeal to conscience. Yet, even with all these odds stacked against such an approach, throughout the entire decade of the 1960s and the first few years of the 1970s, African leaders hardly spoke at these international forums with a united voice. Thus, in the General Assembly proceedings, they have often lined up behind the United States as leader of the West or the Soviet Union as leader of the East, depending on with which bloc they are ideologically associated. Sekou Toure (see extracts from his article 'Africa's Future and the World' in Minogue and Molloy, op. cit., pp. 221–3) has made a succinct historical observation:

Colonialism's greatest misdeed was to have tried to strip us of our responsibility in conducting our own affairs and convince us that our civilization was nothing less than savagery, thus giving us complexes which led to our being branded as irresponsible and lacking in self-confidence.

Of course, in the last few years the picture has been gradually changing. Nonetheless, the question is still relevant as to whether African leaders have shown sufficient foresight, again in the words of Toure, to use their independence as a means of breaking the colonial or neo-colonial system. The answer, in the light of present observation, can be only tentative.

It would seem that African leaders' reliance on international forums is deliberate and in fact masks a certain basic fear. If it can be argued that their rejection of, say, an African Union, is based on a desire to cling to their individual national sovereignties, is it not legitimate to assume that their reliance on international rather than continental forums to solve their development problems is also seen as a way of preserving those sovereignties, since they deal with international forums from a distance without immediate threats?

That this could be so is substantiated by the levity with which African leaders regard the OAU, as evidenced by the uncommonly large number of important issues that are shelved or glossed over when its members meet. The point most stressed by members is the inviolability of national boundaries and sovereignty and in fact the OAU is so structured as to guarantee that very little will be accomplished that does not satisfy every member's bent. A number of questions arise. For instance, is the multiplicity of national entities conducive to African development? Can a continental organisation, built solely on some loose political, rather than economic, notions, be really effective or, for that matter, even worthwhile? Also, is the dualistic (Black and Arab) composition of the organisation not a formula for failure in the pursuit of African aims and aspirations? And, lastly, how independent is the OAU from 'superpower' influence and how sovereign are its members?

Since the Arab oil embargo of 1973, the course of events has changed rapidly for the whole world. The industrial nations have been shocked into a new awareness of the limitations of their economic power and of the mutual dependence between them and the so-called Third World. The Third World itself, rallying behind OPEC (the Organization of Petroleum Exporting Countries), has gained new confidence by realising its economic power and confronting the industrialised world in seeking to fashion a new economic order. The confrontation, observers maintain, is no longer one between East and West, in which the Third World, calling itself non-aligned, plays a neutral role. Rather, it is now a confrontation between the developed (industrialised) and the developing (underdeveloped) countries, or as it is sometimes curiously expressed, between North and South. However, this new division is not as neat as it sounds. It is generally known that following OPEC's oil price increase, Africa, containing a large number of countries, many of them among the poorest, was hit the hardest. A number of these countries were in fact forced to scrap their economic development plans altogether. Although OPEC members have devised some ways of alleviating the African countries' problems, it has been suggested that it will take a number of years for these countries to recover—if indeed recovery is possible—much less make a forward thrust. Thus the OPEC action has exacerbated these problems and also has made more conspicuous the vulnerability of African countries in the face of world economic changes.

On a global level, the OPEC action has also led to a greater coalition of countries for economic self-interests. Thus, the EEC (European Economic Community) and the United States, have come closer to present a united front in their confrontation, not only with oil producers, but with exporters of raw materials in general. The Arab countries, too, who dominate OPEC, have also formed their own sub-unit, the Organization of Arab Petroleum Exporting Countries (OAPEC), thus constituting themselves as a counter-weight to the industrialised nations. But while this is in the general interests of the Third World as a whole, the new economic change poses a special problem for Africa, especially Black Africa, because she now has to deal, from a dependent position, with two economic blocs—the West and the Arabs.

Yet this is ironic when one realises that Africa has the greatest concentration of mineral resources in the world, such as gold, diamonds, copper, iron, phosphates, etc., which together would ordinarily give her a great bargaining leverage with the rest of the world. A continental economic union is, of course, a far, far away idea. But in the absence of such a union, how can Africa best confront the present global economic situation? Can African countries, as individual entities seeking individual interests and advantages, be expected to bargain effectively with the rest of the world in the ensuing struggle for a new economic order? Obviously the answer is no. African countries must unite more strongly and speak more forcefully with one voice. And it is here that the question of the leadership becomes very important and urgent.

WHY NIGERIA?

From the time of independence to the early 1970s, that is, from the civilian administration of Abubakar through the military régime of Gowon, Nigeria played an unenviable role. Despite pleas by many Africans to exert herself more forcefully in the affairs of the continent, in a way commensurate with her population and natural resources, she had played a low-key role that was often interpreted, if not as outright leadership amnesia, then certainly as passivity. It is therefore no wonder that the leadership mantle of the continent was seized by forceful personalities like Kwame Nkrumah of Ghana and Modibo Keita of Mali. While these leaders advocated a more radical approach to such problems as the liberation of Southern Africa from white settlers, and a more radical re-examination of the relationships between independent African States and their former colonial masters, notably France and Britain, Nigeria was seen to be pursuing a course of 'reason-ableness' and 'understanding'—in other words, moderation. While these leaders argued for *real* independence for all Africa, Nigeria was seen to be forging an even closer relationship with Britain and the rest of the West. It was no wonder that, while a leader like Nkrumah was branded a 'Communist dictator', Abubakar was affectionately referred to as 'the Golden Voice of Africa' by the West. Nigeria's stand for moderation was thus perpetuated by the West. Nigeria did not fare much better under Gowon. If Gowon was not the Golden Voice of Africa, he was, at least, admiringly referred to as the 'British-trained' general. And if he improved the continental image of Nigeria, it was never to a degree anticipated by many Nigerians and other Africans, as the country recovered from the wounds of civil war. In fact it was due more to the leadership vacuum that existed in the continent between the overthrow of Nkrumah and the Angolan War of 1975, and certainly not to any new courses charted by him.

So, in the light of her past image, is it not presumptuous to begin to talk about Nigeria's leadership role in Africa today?

What has happened in Nigeria since the exit of Gowon to reverse the position of Nigeria? In other words, why must Nigeria today assume a leadership role in Africa?

There are two things that justify and, in fact, necessitate such a role. The first is the change for the better in her economic situation. This begins with the Arab oil embargo of 1973 and the subsequent increasing of oil prices by OPEC. Whereas in 1972/73, that is the year before the Arab and OPEC action, Nigeria's current revenue was N. 1,277.9 million, this had improved in 1973/74 to N. 1,411.4 million. In 1974/75 when the effect of the oil price increase began to show, current revenue more than doubled to N. 3,121.8 million. By 1975/76 this had increased to N. 5,252.3 million and in 1976/77 it had further increased to N. 6,500 million. In 1977/78 it is expected that this amount will be about N. 7,600 million. This means that Nigeria's GNP has, within the last five years, surpassed that of all other Black African countries combined. Her new development plan for 1975–1980 is expected to involve more than $30 billion. What is significant here, however, is not simply the huge amount, but the proportion that is reflected in external trade, especially with respect to the United States and the rest of the West. Since late 1974, Nigeria has been America's second largest supplier of crude oil. Between 1972 and 1973, American imports of Nigerian oil increased by 84 per cent. The volume of trade with the United States surpassed that between the United States and South Africa in 1974. The United States capital investment in South Africa in 1974 approximated to $1.2 billion and to over $900 million in Nigeria, with this figure expected to increase and to surpass South Africa's over the next few years.

Nigeria's trading position with Great Britain is even more outstanding. It has been well publicised that Nigeria's sterling reserves are so huge that, should she decide to convert them to another currency, the British economy would almost hit the bottom. These brief observations on Nigeria's economic conditions indicate that she, more than any other African country, can best exert leverage on the industrialised West, not only in seeking a new economic order but also in resolving the problems of liberation in Southern Africa.

Nigeria's position *vis-à-vis* OPEC is also unique. Of the thirteen members of OPEC, four—Nigeria, Algeria, Libya and Gabon—are in Africa. Of these, Algeria and Libya, while belonging to the OAU (Organization of African Unity) and having championed the cause of that body, are nonetheless also members of OAPEC (Organization of Arab Petroleum Exporting Countries) and of the Arab League. Thus only Nigeria and Gabon are Black African members of OPEC. In the present relationship between Africa and the Arabs a delicate diplomacy is required. Here, again, Nigeria is in a much stronger position than most African counries to assume leadership of the continent, because of her influence within both OAU and OPEC.

The above brief analysis is no doubt impressive. But the economic indicators so far enumerated were present right from the early seventies. Why is it that only now is there so much talk about Nigeria's leadership role in Africa? Although, during the régime of Gowon, Nigeria began to pay greater and somewhat more visible attention to affairs of the continent, the dramatic metamorphosis of her image could be said to begin with the administration of Murtala Mohammed in 1975 and, more specifically, Nigeria's role in the Angola war of the same year. Her active pro-MPLA stance, and especially her rebuff to the former United States President Ford, who sought to intimidate the OAU members into giving their support to a servile, pro-Western group, was perhaps the most significant event in Nigeria's foreign policy since her independence. Even more significant was her open decision to align herself with progressive forces of the OAU, instead of following her customary bent for consensus. And so, although the vote for recognition of the MPLA was divisive, the victory for the MPLA was nonetheless one of the most generally acclaimed acts of the OAU in its twelve-year history. And of this, Nigeria has every reason to be proud. However, this victory for Nigeria's new foreign policy ironically set such a high level of expectation throughout the continent and abroad that to live up to this, Nigeria must work equally forcefully, without succumbing to external intimidation, on many other fronts.

What I intend to do in this book, then, is to examine some of these other fronts to see what problems may be involved, and how Nigeria could approach them. The first is the OAU itself. This will involve examination of some of the clauses of its charter and possibly its structure. The problems of the OAU are many. Apart from the cultural dualism of its composition, that is, Black–Arab, there is also the Anglophone–Francophone factor. In this chapter it is also relevant, since it involves inter-African relations, to deal with the advantages and problems of Nigeria's wealth. Chapter 2 involves the liberation of Southern Africa, and this chapter is obviously closely connected with the first. Here, however, I examine how Nigeria can use her economic and political strength to deal with foreign nations—the United States and the West and the Soviet Union and the East—all of whom have great potential in either solving or complicating the problems of that region of Africa. Chapter 5 is devoted to African–Arab relations. This again is closely connected with the first two chapters. And finally, some inquiry is made into the affairs of the international organisations and their relevance to the development programmes of African countries.

2 Clearing away the Illusions

In a broadcast to the nation on 29 June 1976, the Head of State, General Obasanjo, identified 'the permanent and fundamental foreign policy objectives' of the country, as follows:

(i) The defence of our sovereignty, independence and territorial integrity.

(ii) The creation of the necessary political and economic conditions in Africa and in the rest of the world which would foster Nigerian national self-reliance and rapid economic development. This would facilitate the defence of the independence of all African countries.

(iii) The promotion of equality and self-reliance in Africa and the rest of the developing world.

(iv) The promotion and defence of social justice and respect for human dignity, especially the dignity of the Black man.

(v) The promotion and defence of world peace.

Some of these objectives are close to, or in fact embrace, some of the arguments that we hope to make here. But having argued that Nigeria is best qualified to take Africa's leadership mantle, it is only appropriate that we devote a few pages to indicating some of the limits of her power. It is a clearing away of illusions, if you like, because in the present atmosphere of dizziness caused, no doubt, by her new wealth, she is susceptible to a lot of distortions about herself. Some of these distortions may be internally generated, whilst others are certainly imposed from the outside.

The latter kind of distortion may derive from foreign press reports and from the hard statistical figures which each foreign paper or journal or broadcast may use in support of the perceived image of its country. For example we may read (*Africa Report* Vol. 22, May–June 1977, No. 3), that 'As Black Africa's richest and most populous nation with a $27 billion GDP in 1976 spread over a population of 70–80 million people . . .' or (*Foreign Affairs*, Vol. 1, January 1975), '. . . Nigeria is powerful in Africa. Its army, mobilized originally against the Biafran secession, still stands at some 250,000. It is the largest by far in Black Africa, four times the size of the next, that of Zaire . . .' and ' . . . Nigeria's Head of State has been enthusiastically received on state visits to Britain, the Soviet Union, and mainland China . . .'. We may even read about hard statistics concerning her development plans, such as 'Nigeria's Third National Development Plan, 1975–1980, could call for anywhere between $48 and $70 billion in development expenditures . . .' and that Nigeria's trade with the United States is surpassing that between the latter and South Africa.

On the home front, too, we are not only exposed to daily reports about how well our country may be doing, and doing in comparison with others in the continent, but the evidence may be readily available to support our notions. However, the danger is that while all we read—whether in the foreign or home press—and all we see, may be true, it is never the whole truth. And even less true is the notion that such wealth, the object of our euphoria, can alone make for leadership. Hence this chapter is not so much about how large is Nigeria's GDP, as how well it is used at home. This is important because leadership abroad can never be sustained or successful unless it is complemented by good leadership at home, i.e., leadership supported by all the people. And those who may be cynical about this need only take an example from the United States, a country that is immensely wealthy and powerful. When the US entered South-East Asia in the early sixties she did so amid general support from home because the people thought 'they' had vital interests to defend there and a moral responsibility to defend their Asian allies. But when Americans felt that their wealth was in fact being squandered abroad only for the benefit and interests of a few corporations, and not for the benefit and interest of 'all' and that the home front was being ignored, with decaying cities uncared for, the government was brought down amid cries of 'foul'. Thus the neglect of the home front undercut America's leadership abroad and very soon she was despised by even those who she purported to defend or help. In the same way, in her leadership role in Africa, Nigeria will be judged more by how well she keeps her own house in order.

Fortunately, this fact has been recognised by the External Affairs Commissioner, Brigadier Joseph Garba, who, on 19 February 1977, in his address at the University of Ibadan, on 'Foreign Policy and the Problems of Economic Development', said:

> It is perfectly legitimate for you to pose the question as to the relationship between foreign policy and the national objective of rapid and judicious economic and social progress. I would first of all say with all the conviction that I can muster that no nation can effectively pursue a dynamic and independent foreign policy with a weak and dependent economy. Indeed, I would go as far as to declare that Nigeria's ability to succeed in her diplomatic endeavours will, to a large extent, depend on her economic strength.

Now, where does she begin to learn her lessons?

The first is, obviously, in the area of the distribution of her wealth. 'Distribution', of course, is a scare-word among Nigerians, as it suggests to them the hydra of 'communism' or 'socialism'. But it should suggest neither this nor the robbing of Peter to pay Paul, as long as Peter had not robbed Paul in the first place. Here we are concerned about equality of opportunity for all and a clear satisfaction for all that the country's wealth is visibly transforming all citizens' lives and not merely those of the few distant 'them'.

The Head of State, Lt-General Obasanjo, has already touched on the first in his so-called 'Dodan Declaration' of 1 January 1977:

> We cannot afford to build a nation in which a handful of people exclusively own and control the means of production and distribution to the perpetual detriment of the majority. That will be creating conflicts which will sooner or later disrupt economic and social progress. In days gone by in most of our traditional societies, the working group accepted responsibility for the economic and social welfare of the people. We therefore have no cause today under any guise to forsake the even-handed treatment and welfare of the majority of our people. We must all rededicate ourselves anew to the tasks of reducing the mental and material hardship brought on fellow Nigerians by artificial scarcity, poor means of distribution, greed, selfishness and minority control of resources belonging rightly to all Nigerians.

These laudable remarks which emphasise only the production and distribution control question lead us to the second aspect of the problem. In a country like Nigeria, where there are so many illiterates who do not understand business procedures, and many more who may not know their way to a bank to get the loan, how can we talk about equal opportunity in production and distribution? But here I am not advocating strict capitalism or strict socialism; rather I am urging a synthesis of the two. For, in fact, as the Head of State has pointed out, in African tradition capitalism and socialism are not necessarily incompatible. They should operate in good balance: capitalism for the means of production, socialism (or communalism) in the enjoyment of the fruits. In other words, our argument is not against capitalism. Rather, since all people do not have access to the means of production, the responsibility falls on the government to ensure that even those who do not have such access see around them in their villages or in their farms improvements in their lives brought about by the 'Petronaira'. Only then will they support, or even tolerate, the country giving aid to outsiders. Only then will they support or even tolerate her leadership role.

There is also the question of sincerity and honesty. Of course, the question may be posed as to what morality has to do with Nigeria's leadership role in Africa. Yet it must be stressed that, of all the problems that will confront any country in her march towards economic, political and social development, none is as dangerous or as forbidding as that of the leadership appearing to be corrupt or deceitful. In fact, corruption and deceitfulness at the top may be so corrosive to the national well-being that it would be folly to talk about leadership abroad. This involves two aspects of the same thing. Corruption we all know about. It involves money and services. Either it is an outright embezzlement or stealing from a position of responsibility—whether the position is high or low—or it is obtaining money for services not rendered, or for services rendered in the line of duty which, under normal circumstances, do not require any extra personal remuneration. Thus the postal clerk or the telephone exchange man demands 'something' before one's letter is properly stamped and mailed or before one's call is put through. Or the customs or immigration clerk demands a 'dash' before one's luggage is passed through or so that he may look the other way while illegal goods pass through. The hoarder may create artificial scarcity so that he can reap greater profits, or the contractor may use inferior material where he is already contracted to use a better material. Or he may even spend the money without producing the product for which he is contracted. All these are forms of corruption that destroy the national social fabric and should be stamped out by every means possible. Yet none of these would be seen by the citizenry to be as corrosive to the national well-being as when practised by the leadership, for only then does corruption become a national trademark. That is debilitating to the country's leadership role in the continent.

Bad as corruption is, however, it is perhaps even less destructive to a country's well-being than deceitfulness. Deceitfulness comes in two forms; it is like a double-barrelled gun. But it does not shoot from one direction; it blasts from two opposite directions. In the first instance, we are talking about deceitfulness at home, about promises unfulfilled. We have seen examples of corruption and this kind of deceitfulness in the Gowon régime. Development projects are promised, but the promises are unfulfilled. A restructuring of the political system is promised but never happens. Most importantly, the leadership says it wants to move the country in a certain direction, but in fact allows it to move in another direction.

On the other hand, deceitfulness could also apply in the country's external relations. It then invariably involves either political weakness, in terms of delivering what is promised abroad; or it could derive from sheer illusion about the country's capabilities, so that promises made cannot be fulfilled. The result is that, at home, there will be turmoil when the people know that the country is forcing itself to honour promises abroad at their expense. And if the people prevail, then the country becomes an object of ridicule abroad. None of these situations makes for a successful leadership role.

Hence it is necessary, before making promises and luxuriating in our sudden wealth, to remove all illusions and to have a definite idea of the country's ability abroad in her leadership role.

The people must constantly be made to understand that by any standards Nigeria is still a poor and underdeveloped country. If we use the old yardstick of per capita income, it will be discovered that Nigeria is still far below a number of other African countries, such as Libya, Morocco, Tunisia, Gabon, Ivory Coast or Ghana. But even if we agree with modern economists, who are beginning to reject this form of measurement, it will still be seen that the country's present so-called affluence is only relative to the poverty of so many other African countries. Therefore the people must be reminded not to live and think as if Nigeria were a land of milk and honey. The illusion of a 'rich' country breeds unnecessary arrogance and unnecessary arrogance toward outsiders in the continent would not be productive in playing a leadership role.

The leadership must also spell out clearly to the people the purpose of all aid given to any African country. This would prevent unnecessary speculation and misconceptions at home. But most importantly, the leadership must stress to the people that the purpose of any such aid is not primarily to win over the recipient country as a client or as a puppet. The examples of the superpowers—the United States and the Union of Soviet Socialist Republics—are lessons enough for us all that aid given under such terms is destructive, rather than productive, of leadership roles. Nigeria must play her leadership game by the rules for which she censures other big powers. This point cannot be over-emphasised. There is no continent in which the term 'leadership role' is looked upon with more suspicion than in Africa. Not only are individual leaders extremely jealous of their powers because of the prestige attached to such power, but they are perhaps justifiably wary of the term because of their experiences throughout the history of their nations, with colonialism and the superpowers. She must therefore not act like a colonial power and transparent hypocrisy on her part would only tip the balance against her.

There is a tendency for Nigerians to think, perhaps in the light of the country's GDP and the strength of her standing army, that Nigeria can duplicate America's world role in a miniature form in the continent; that is, the role of a continental policeman. But experts have stressed that in the next decade or decade and a half, even with her present wealth, Nigeria will not be able to dominate the affairs of the continent either politically or militarily. She simply will not have the resources to do so. And even if she had them, to attempt such a course without selectivity would be not only a waste to the country itself, but also the surest way to invite hostility towards herself. The leadership, therefore, whilst it must listen to the voices and opinions of the people, must not let itself and the country be swayed into unrealistic and arrogant continental power-play.

Obviously some of these points may be seen to stem from

morality, and every man in the street has been told so often by learned men that morality and politics or diplomacy do not mix. But again, we have to take an example from the United States to see that while this is true most of the time, either at home or abroad, yet somewhere along the line in the course of history, even powerful states and leaders have been brought down by the absence of morality. They are invariably rejected or scorned. Therefore, for Nigeria to be accepted as a leader in the continent, her actions both at home and abroad, while politically expedient, must also be fair.

3 Nigeria, the OAU and the Continental Interest

To understand the basic structure of the Organization of African Unity (OAU) and some of its current problems, it is necessary to know how the Organization came into existence. If one may be pardoned for indulging in a semantic exercise, the name, Organization of African Unity, with its emphasis on *Unity*, may give us some clue as to the thinking of those African leaders who met in Addis Ababa in 1963 to inaugurate the Organization. For instance, why was it called Organization of African *Unity* rather than, say, Organization of African States? What is the historical significance of this?

The period immediately preceding the establishment of the OAU was characterised by regionalism, factionalism and raucous ideological warfare among leaders. This chaos was epitomised in the Congo crisis of 1960–62, when the continent was sharply divided in its opinion on how best the crisis could be resolved, not by Africans, but by external powers through the organ of the United Nations. In its response to this situation, the continent was split into three groups or factions: the Brazzaville Group (which felt that the UN should have minimised its involvement in the crisis); the Casablanca Group (which felt UN intervention was initially insufficient); and the Monrovia/Lagos Group (which seemed satisfied with the UN's role in the crisis). The dangers inherent in this divisiveness were clear to most leaders and when Emperor Haile Selassie, during the 1961 UN General Assembly Debate, called upon sister African States to come together to save the continent from the imminent threat of East–West Cold War destructiveness, it was on the rationalisation that African problems could best be solved by Africans themselves, free from outside influence or pressure.

The establishment of the OAU was also influenced by the determination of the leaders of the 29 independent states to see decolonised the non-self-governing territories, and particularly to work for the liberation of Black Southern Africa from the oppression of white minority regimes.

The formation of the OAU was thought to be the best way of overcoming the rifts which had become embarrassingly obvious during the Congo crisis. But the source of the ideological rift was not limited to the Congo crisis: there was the war in Algeria between France and the Algerian Liberation Front; there was the problem of Mauritania; and also the general question of safeguarding African interests in the world. By the end of 1961 the various factions had consolidated themselves into two major groups: the Casablanca, consisting of the six West African and North African States (Ghana, Guinea, Mali, Morocco, Egypt and the Algerian Liberation Front)—a group regarded as generally radical and progressive; and the Monrovia, which consisted of a collection of moderate to conservative states. Bringing such vehemently opposed groups together was difficult enough. What added to the difficulty was the Brazzaville Group, whose members, though ostensibly subsumed into the Monrovia Group, nonetheless kept a distinct identity within and outside it. Also exacerbating this problem were the facts that its membership was linguistically defined and that it had a colonial link with France. The Brazzaville Group consisted of Cameroon, the Central African Republic, Chad, Congo (Brazzaville), Dahomey, Gabon, Ivory Coast, Madagascar, Mauritania, Niger, Senegal and Upper Volta. In other words, the Brazzaville Group was a purely Francophone creature. One of the most difficult problems confronting the founders of the OAU was how to tackle the issue of regionalism or 'bloc-ism', whether based on cultural, linguistic, geographic, or colonial affinity. Although the Casablanca and Monrovia Groups were abolished, the Brazzaville Group became intransigent. It created a division within the OAU, between itself and the rest of the African States. First, it functioned as a political grouping within the Organization, and then, when pressure from the Organization's majority members became intense, it formed itself into an economic unit. But again, in the mid-sixties, when the issue of interference in the internal affairs of states became prominent, the Group resurfaced as a political force.

Although, for a while, the issue took a back seat, an intelligent guess would indicate that the manoeuvrings and hagglings that it initially generated led to some indefensible compromises in the drafting of the Organization's charter. In fact, Berhanykun Andemicael (*The OAU and the UN*, New York: UNITAR/Africana Publishing Co., 1976, pp. 9–24) has noted that at first the founders of the Organization did not raise the issue of sub-regionalism. Such compromise, or even appeasement, would also indicate that a number of the African States did not consider the establishment of the OAU with as much enthusiasm and interest as one would have expected. Perhaps it was caution against creating any continental superstructure which might encroach on the hard-won sovereignty of their respective states. Whatever the reason, the result was the creation of an almost powerless Organization, particularly in relation to intervention in the so-called internal affairs of individual member states. Thus the most significant source of the weakness of the OAU could be traced to this yoking together of both nationalist and pan-Africanist sentiments in a pact of imbalance, in which nationalism is allowed to supersede continental interests. This, perhaps, is what Ali Mazrui had in mind when he remarked that the Organization was based only on the sentiment 'We are all Africans' and on a bogus pan-African ideal of 'racial sovereignty' (see Leon Gordenker's essay in Mazrui and Patel (eds.) *Africa in World Affairs*, (New York: The Third Press, 1972) pp. 109–10.)

It has been quite a long time since 1963. In 1961 when Haile Selassie called for the creation of an organisation of African States:

. . . the basic and fundamental task of which will be to furnish the mechanism whereby problems which arise on the continent and which are of primary interest to the region could, in the first instance, be dealt with by Africans, in an African forum, free from outside influence and pressure. (United Nations General Assembly Official Records, 16th Session, 1020th Plenary Meeting, 2 October 1961, p. 177)

he could be said to be thinking mainly of political problems. Although in the drafting of the charter, some attention was also paid to economic and social issues, the Organization has functioned somewhat in the spirit of Selassie's thinking. Not only that, but as the Organization evolved over the years, its energy was concentrated on the issues of decolonisation and liberation, the only two aspects of the Organization's role about which there seems to be agreement amongst the states. The above issues, however, have also been intermittently disrupted and even pushed out of focus by the vexing problems of inter-state and intra-national disputes and wars. As other pressing problems plaguing the continent begin to emerge more clearly, and frustration begins to rise over the OAU's inability to deal with them, it has become increasingly necessary to re-examine the Organization with regard to its basic principles, its charter and its administrative structure; in fact, to question whether it has any basis for existence at all, and if so, what its future will be.

Earlier, we referred to Mazrui's remark that the Organization is based on mere sentiment. Others, such as Andemicael and Gordenker, have been a little kinder. Gordenker (*Africa in World Affairs*, op. cit., pp. 109–10), while noting that 'the poverty-stricken Governments of the least developed part of the world' could hardly be expected to create an organisation for a military purpose, nonetheless argues that it would be absurd to have such a continental organisation for none other than sentimental reasons. Sadly, however, Gordenker and others who take this view seem to concern themselves with such issues as the relationship between the OAU and the UN and whether or not the former, in its present goals, aims, principles, and structure, can in fact coexist with the latter. They point out that the OAU owes its existence to the UN clause and is in fact modelled upon it. The result is that the successes and failures of the OAU are examined in the light of the successes and failures of the UN. Thus, if the UN is useful and necessary as a universal organisation, its offshoot, the OAU, must be just as useful and necessary as a regional subsidiary.

If either of the above reasonings, that is, Mazrui's or Gordenker's, is true, then a number of questions must be answered. For instance, if it were true that the OAU were based on some ideology of 'racial sovereignty' how could this be explained by its Black–Arab composition? Indeed, if that were so, would it not be a reasonable assumption that the Organization could actually have functioned much better than it has done so far? And on the other hand, if the OAU has taken the United Nations as its model, could this perhaps explain its failure to date? This argument can be pushed a little further if, as I do, we reject the notion that the establishment of the OAU was influenced by any coherent ideology. The problems that have plagued the OAU, most experts would agree, are not peculiar to it. Rather, on a general level, they are the same problems that have afflicted other regional or continental groupings in the Third World – the Organization of American States, the South and East Asia groups and even the Arab League. Why are these groupings less successful than, say, the EEC (European Economic Community)? Is it not reasonable to argue that the failure of the Third-World groupings has been due mainly to the fact that they are a mélange of nations with a variety of views, without a unifying ideology, whereas the unity and the success of the EEC is due largely to the coherence of its ideological make-up? In other words, is it not possible that the failure of these regional groupings, particularly of the OAU, is a failure in the absence of a unifying ideology? (Those who might disagree with this hypothesis might do well to re-examine Dr Nkrumah's argument on the need for this kind of ideology as a prerequisite of a functional continental union.)

In any case, if any of these suppositions is even partly true, then neither of the two arguments we began with entirely explains a justifiable basis for the existence of the OAU.

Another criticism aimed at the Organization concerns its priorities. Some scholars have derisively remarked that, while an organisation like the EEC began by laying the economic foundation of its region, and is only now moving towards political union, the OAU is moving in the opposite direction: that is, beginning with a political aim, and no clear programme for economic or social development; that even the political agenda is circumscribed by the narrow aims of decolonisation and of the inviolability of the sovereignty of states. On a certain level, of course, this comparison is somewhat unfair. The most pressing problem of Western Europe after the devastation caused by the Second World War was economic reconstruction. For Africa, and the OAU, the priority was different, and throughout this entire half-century the over-riding problem has been the need to be free from foreign rule, whether in Southern Africa or in other former colonial territories.

While all the above criticisms require careful attention, the most significant and persistent attack on the OAU has been directed against its charter and its structure. Why?

We have already noted the basic weaknesses that have their origin in the Organization's history. Andemicael (op. cit., p. 15) has indicated some of the peculiarities of the OAU, that is, characteristics which distinguish it from other regional organisations such as the Organization of American States or the League of Arab States. The OAU, he points out, is the only regional organisation which, although its *raison d'être* is to resolve conflicts and disputes, has neither the necessary disciplinary power over member states nor the mechanism to repulse outside aggression. Another aspect of this inbuilt mechanism for failure is the refusal of the Organization to give its secretary-general or its Commission of Mediation, Conciliation and Arbitration the power to initiate a dialogue with the parties to a dispute, where it is felt that such a dialogue could prevent the dispute from accelerating. In other words, the OAU is the only regional organisation which denies its secretary-general any kind of political initiative whatsoever.

Another criticism levelled at the OAU concerns its over-emphasis on non-interference and the inviolability of states' boundaries. To be more specific, let us examine some of the principles and articles of the OAU. Here, I think it will be useful to go back to the earlier arguments of advocates of a strong Pan-Africa, men such as Nkrumah and Azikiwe. In his book, *I Talk of Freedom* (1961), Nkrumah, speaking of the balkanisation of the continent into a multiplicity of unviable States, emphasised that:

> . . . These States are designed to be so weak and unstable in the organization of their national economies and administrations that they will be compelled by internal as well as external pressures to continue to depend upon the colonial powers who have ruled them for several years. The weaker and less stable an African State is, the easier it is for the colonial power concerned to dominate the affairs and fortunes of the new State, even though it is supposed to have gained independence.

Samir Amin has also made the same point with his analysis of the Gambia. In the light of this, it is curious to see the great emphasis which the OAU charter places on the questions of national sovereignty and the inviolability of states:

PRINCIPLES: Article III
The Member States, in pursuit of the purposes stated in Article II, solemnly affirm and declare their adherence to the following principles:
1. The sovereignty and equality of all African and Malagasy States.
2. Non-interference in the internal affairs of States.
3. Respect for the sovereignty and territorial integrity of

each State and for its inalienable right to independent existence.

4. Peaceful settlement of disputes by negotiation, mediation, conciliation or arbitration.

5. Unreserved condemnation, in all its forms, of political assassination as well as of subversive activities on the part of neighbouring States or any other States.

6. Absolute dedication to the total emancipation of the African territories which are still dependent.

7. Affirmation of a policy of non-alignment with regard to all blocs.

It is to be observed that the all principles underlying the establishment of the Organization, except for the last two, are concerned primarily with the protection of individual states against interference in their internal affairs by other states. Thus, in effect, the OAU charter is nothing but a perpetuation of the colonial heritage. Of course, it can be argued that it makes room for states to federate, should they wish to do so and, moreover, that no state can be forced to federate with another against her will. But to any reasonable mind, this provision appears to be nothing more than an afterthought, since the Organization's attitude to this problem is so vague and so neutral that it tends rather to discourage any such coming-together of states. Is it not reasonable to believe that it would be infinitely more fruitful for the Organization to create incentives, say, through political and economic support, for member states to federate. Instead, it can be observed that, since independence, any such attempted federation has generated hostility and contempt from neighbouring states, who see such a coming-together as a threat to their own national sovereignty. Examples abound: the Ghana–Guinea–Mali federation of Nkrumah/Toure/Keita days, although it had its enemies within, was plagued with problems right from the beginning, because of the hostility of neighbouring states. The United Arab federation is another attempt which died of the same causes. Even the most recent of these attempts, the

Libya–Tunisia federation, whose pact was scuttled before it even left the drawing board, failed almost entirely as a result of the open hostility of Egypt, Algeria and Morocco, who saw it as an attempt to wreck the political alignment of states in that region of the continent. This, in spite of the fact that a good percentage of the top-level segment of the Libyan labour force is composed of Egyptians! Is it wrong, then, to assume that one of the greatest obstacles to African unity and consequent economic development is the selfish motivation of leaders to preserve their individual powers, overriding the economic interests of their peoples?

The issue of non-interference is, on a certain level, even more inimical to the political and economic interests of the continent. For the fact that most of these states—both large and small—are not economically viable, and therefore are politically unstable, means that they will continually (as long as they remain so) exist by sufferance of the affluent and industrialised countries of the West and East. Thus, the sovereignty they so jealously guard is nothing more, in Nkrumah's words, than 'Conditional Independence'. In his book, *I Talk of Freedom*, Nkrumah wrote about this phenomenon:

> . . . As independent States, these territories are supposed to acquire international personality and establish diplomatic relations with other States and also have representation in various international organizations, including the United Nations. Once this stage has been reached, the devil of colonialism will put all its energies into establishing control over the foreign relations and policies of the new African States.

This means that, while the OAU is obsessed with the issue of interference by neighbouring African states, it inadvertently or deliberately sanctions foreign interference on two levels. The first involves what we have already called 'conditional independence', whereby a non-viable state willingly lets a former colonial master set the guidelines for its behaviour. The second, more open and cruder, involves the former colonial master who, under cover of discharging her responsibilities to a former client, intervenes militarily on behalf of that client against another state, with whom the former has a dispute. The result is that, no matter who wins in the dispute, both states have lost their independence and self-respect—to the detriment of the continent as a whole. This phenomenon does not end here. In time, both states fall back on the support of outside protectors and the arms race begins, with each protector piling up deadly arms in their respective 'client' states. This is not a fantasy scenario. It is already taking place all over the continent.

Africa saw an example of this in the then Congo, where outside interests pressured one of her wealthiest provinces, Katanga, to secede so that they could more easily control her wealth. The loss of Prime Minister Patrice Lumumba is today the loss of the continent as a whole. In the mid-sixties we saw the same intrigue played in Nigeria, where a civil war which was caused by the genuine feelings of hurt by one region, was soon internationalised in such a way that certain foreign powers, particularly France, became nefariously interested in balkanising the country so as to make her more amenable to control and less of a threat to neighbouring client states. A recent example is seen in Ethiopia, where Eritrea, instead of working to make Ethiopia as a whole a more viable country, to the benefit of all her peoples, is waging a secession war with the active support of Somalia, Sudan, Egypt, Saudi Arabia, and other Arab states outside the continent. And not only the Arab countries are involved. Gradually the entire Horn of Africa has become a superpower theatre for destruction as each side appeals to its protector for arms.

Of all these recent examples of foreign interference, perhaps the most flagrant and the most humiliating were two involving Zaire first in 1977 and again in 1978. In the first, Zaire, unable to defend herself, appealed to foreign powers. Not only did Morocco, Egypt and Syria rush forward with arms and men under the guise of protecting neighbouring Sudan, but France and Belgium—both former colonial masters—saw themselves as having responsibility to defend Zaire, although in fact their interest was purely mercenary, to protect their investments in Zaire with particular regard to Zairian copper. Thereafter, France hurriedly convened a conference of all her former colonies, at which she boldly reassured them that she would discharge her responsibility towards them in the same flagrant way she had acted in the case of Zaire. And to show that she could make good her word, France recently arrogantly revealed another area of intervention on African soil, in the border clash between Chad and Libya (*International Herald Tribune*, 20 July 1977).

In all these instances of foreign interference and deliberate sabotage of the interests and vitality of the continent, the OAU has emerged looking more ineffectual than a toothless bulldog. The power vacuum created by the OAU has allowed some of the Western countries to act hypocritically by almost invariably defending discredited leaders and maintaining them in power, always from a selfish motive. But it should also be made clear that I am not here advocating a double standard of peace and justice, whereby I condemn the intervention of big powers in the affairs of the continent, while at the same time condoning or encouraging the bellicosity of some African states against others. What I have tried to indicate is simply that the OAU's emphasis on non-interference even by the OAU itself in the affairs of an African state is neither a safeguard against intra-national wars and disputes nor, for that matter, a blow in favour of the sovereignty of individual states. Rather, it invites international interference by competing outside powers. Moreover, by failing to distinguish between 'external interference' and 'interference' by the citizens for the reason of removing an unwanted leader, the OAU unwittingly joins the West in thwarting the aspirations of the masses of Africa.

Again, it will of course be argued that the OAU has been working tirelessly to minimise these intra-African wars or that it is powerless, in the absence of a Continental Military Command, to do anything. But if the former is true, then the effort has been overshadowed by the cries of 'Sovereignty of states! Inviolability of national boundaries!' If the latter is the case, then should not the Organization re-examine the Charter articles which deal with this problem? The Organization should understand that the violation of national boundaries is not always bad; more importantly, it should be realised that interference need not be through force of arms alone. For instance, in the case of a civil war, would interference not be useful if it were in the form of a collective effort to dissuade seceding enclaves or provinces from embarking on destructive ventures, or in serving notice to a recalcitrant party that it can expect no help from any part of the continent? If the OAU had sent representatives to Nigeria before the civil war to dissuade Ojukwu from embarking on a dangerous course and if Nigeria had not blocked such an initiative by citing the principle of non-interference (even by the OAU) in her internal affairs, is it not reasonable to assume that perhaps the civil war could have been avoided?

Again, in the case of the East African Horn, would it not be a useful act, and thus beneficial to the continent, if the OAU were to support the Soviet Union—(forget, for the moment, her ulterior motives) in persuading Ethiopia (that is including Eritrea), Somalia and Yemen to federate, instead of the three waging an internecine war which will end up in further balkanisation of the region?

Another unique characteristic of the OAU concerns its charter article on membership. This stipulates that any independent African state automatically becomes a member unless she does not wish to do so. Moreover, there is no clause in the charter which allows for the removal or suspension of a member state from the Organization, should that state fail to live up to its ideals. Is the rationale for these aberrations that of 'we are all Africans' and therefore no one should be excluded? Or did the writers of the charter really believe that such lapses would work in the interests of the continent? Is it not reasonable to assume that the threat of expulsion, and thus of isolation, could act as a deterrent against individual heads of state who might wish to embark on reprehensible acts against their own people?

Yet, the reality of the situation is that the OAU, in order to present to the world an outward appearance of unity, is often seen to apply an embarrassing double standard in judging issues that perennially plague it—one for African leaders, the other for non-Africans. Thus, the Organization, or several of its members, will enthusiastically condemn the reprehensible acts committed by outsiders, such as the United States' involvement in Vietnam and Cambodia, while the same bestiality committed by an Amin of Uganda, a Micombero of Burundi or an Nguema of Equatorial Guinea, against their own peoples, is greeted with shameless silence under the facade of not wishing to wash Africa's dirty linen in public.

The above criticism inevitably draws attention to an interrelated defect in the charter. This is being belatedly recognised by scholars, who point out that while the charter is obsessively concerned with the protection of states and individual leaders (is it therefore a wonder that most of the African leaders equate themselves with the state?), it is embarrassingly silent on the protection of individual citizens. Thus, any leader who takes it into his head to vent his spleen on his own citizens on a murderous scale can do so without fear of interference in his internal affairs by the OAU.

Two final problems of the OAU have nothing to do with the charter itself, but they are perhaps the most intractable to resolve. Both have their source in history and culture. The first is what might properly be called the Anglo-Francophone factor. Most African scholars are agreed that the linguistic division in the continent between English-speaking and French-speaking is one of the most dangerous and destructive factors in Africa's search for unity and development. The language issue itself poses a paradox in the continent. On the one hand, we realise that the problem of cultural and linguistic multiplicity existed in Africa long before the white man forced

Africans to learn English and French. So the white man (or colonialism) cannot be blamed for having invented it. In fact, the forced adoption of these colonial languages could be said to have brought a certain amount of unity in colonial times. The paradox is that in the post-independence era these very languages, which once served the continent well, are the very source of its disharmony. What we are talking about here is really more than mere linguistic division; we are talking about the effects of our entire colonial history. With respect to continental unity, and particularly to the OAU, this takes us back to the problem cited earlier concerning the fragmentation of the continent into three hostile ideological factions during the Congo crisis and the subsequent manoeuvrings attendant on the establishment of the Organization. As we indicated, the Brazzaville Group, which later constituted itself into the Organization Commune Africaine, Malagasy et Mauritiene (OCAM), was specifically French-speaking. Throughout the entire history of the OAU, with the refusal of this sub-group to disappear, the animosity originally generated has led to persistent rivalry between Francophone and Anglophone Africa. This rivalry has been so disruptive within the Organization that sometimes it makes a meeting between fellow Africans seem more like a confrontation between two quarrelling racial groups, each seeking to assert its superiority over the other. Such rivalry, on a certain level, might be tolerable and even useful to national and continental interests, by injecting some dynamism into the proceedings. Unfortunately, no such useful purpose has been served in this context, not even for self-aggrandisement. Rather, it would appear to serve only to preserve the hegemony of former colonial masters within the continent. Senegal, in particular, is willing to veto any kind of cooperation between French-speaking and English-speaking states if she suspects that such cooperation is likely to reduce the influence of France within the continent. Senegal's recent acceptance of the Economic Commission of West African States (ECOWAS) was more the result of her fear of isolation within West Africa than of any genuine desire for such cooperation. Even her insistence on bringing Zaire (a state in Central Africa) into the Community (of West African States) was a destructive tactical move. In general, the suspicion between the French-speaking and English-speaking states is so great that serious issues of mutual, and thus continental, concern are often left unresolved.

One of the earliest issues to divide Africa on a scale almost equal to that of the Congo crisis, was the French atomic test carried out in the Sahara. The call by many African states to sever diplomatic relations with France, or at least in some way to show Africa's anger, was undercut by the unanimous opposition of the Francophone states. Nigeria, amongst a few other African states who dared to oppose France, was for years punished by France for this opposition, as was shown by her veto of Nigeria's admission into associate membership of the EEC.

Another such divisive issue has been France's economic, technical and military relationship with South Africa. Although it has been known for years that France has openly defied the UN's call to member states to refrain from collaboration with apartheid South Africa, the OAU has found it impossible to pass a resolution condemning her. In fact, under the suspected backing of the United States, France and other European powers, a number of African countries— specifically Ivory Coast, Senegal and Sierra Leone—have flouted the OAU resolutions dissuading any dialogue with the Vorster régime. The English-speaking countries, on their part, have not been totally blameless, as was shown by the 1963 unilateral declaration of independence by the white minority in Rhodesia and Britain's refusal to bring the rebels to heel. Here it could be argued that the English-speaking nations did not show the same degree of boldness in confronting Britain that they directed against France during the atomic test crisis. Nonetheless, it would be agreed that overall, the English-speaking states have shown greater independence and a greater detachment from Britain than the French-speaking states in dealing with those issues which specifically concern the continent.

The most recent instance of this division involves the Francophone participation—to the embarrassment of the rest of the Continent—in the Paris Conference and support for a NATO-sponsored All-Africa Force.

Two results of this divisiveness have been:

(1) The OAU has been weakened since it can never hope to pass any resolution which will be adhered to by all members; and

(2) Each member state is thus vulnerable to the wrath of any big power, as the Nigeria–France example has shown, since she cannot act in the full assurance of the backing of the other member states.

Yet another area of potential divisiveness within the OAU involves what we might call the Black–Arab factor. For years, most members of the OAU did not want to admit openly that any problem existed here. Some have even argued that, if any problem existed, it was no worse than that caused by the Franco–Anglophone factor. This may be largely true, particularly since the Franco–Anglophone problem is not limited to Black Africa but extends through Arab Africa also. While I intend to discuss the Black–Arab issue more fully in Chapter 5, let us raise some preliminary questions here as they pertain to the workings of the OAU.

For instance: (1) If it is true, as Ali Mazrui has indicated earlier, that the OAU is based on (a) the feeling that 'we are all Africans'; and (b) the Pan-African ideal of 'racial sovereignty', then does this not imply that the OAU was founded on two contradictory concepts? (2) Or do we take the term 'racial sovereignty' to mean Black and Arab? These questions are pertinent because of the relationship between the OAU and the League of Arab States and the peculiar dual membership of the North African Arab States in both organisations.

Obviously, most leaders would prefer to remain silent on this issue. But if these questions seem divisive, we only have to refer to the recent battle during FESTAC between Senghor (Senegal) and Nigeria over the issue of whether or not Arabs should be admitted to participate in the Symposium on Black Culture. If nothing else, this disagreement indicated the necessity of sooner or later resolving the Black–Arab question, if the relationship is to prosper at all. Let it be on record, however, that I do not doubt that this type of dualism within the OAU could be beneficial to the Organization. The recent meeting between the two organisations in Cairo has shown this to be so. However, it is a double-edged sword, and on the whole seems merely to have generated the kind of problems that go with serving two masters. One of the major problems has been the suspicion among Black Africans that the Arab States do not have a sincere interest in the affairs of the OAU and Black Africa beyond obtaining their support for the Palestinian question. There is, of course, some generalisation here, since some of the Arab States—for example Algeria—are undoubtedly committed to the problems of the continent. In the light of all these problems it would seem reasonable to suggest that the OAU should re-examine itself and to re-define or clarify the basic principles and beliefs which make it an all-embracing organisation.

Having indicated some of the problems which affect the organisation, the question now is: How can Nigeria contribute in the effort to seek solutions? Obviously, the problems that will confront her in any attempt to exercise leadership are many and complex. Her past passivity will undoubtedly count against her, but this need not be an insurmountable obstacle.

I have already made some suggestions concerning the OAU charter and its principles. There is little more that Nigeria can do in this regard other than examining them and, if she finds them worthwhile, pushing for them with all her might.

Another problem derives from the fact that she is a newcomer into the sweepstakes game of leadership politics. And here she has two rivals to contend with: (1) Senegal (under Senghor) as a philosophical leader of the French-speaking states and (2) Algeria, as the ideological aspirant to the Third-World leadership role. Throughout her years of independence Nigeria has shown no zeal for either philosophy or ideology. Therefore she must wage her battle on a territory where she is more sure of her potential, that is, on the plane of economic and human resources. With her present economic capacity she has more leverage in the leadership game than any other country in the continent. Her role in the establishment of ECOWAS already indicates that, with tact, she can overcome the obstacles created by linguistic divisiveness. But ECOWAS is not enough. She must patiently, but rigorously, cultivate closer ties with other French-speaking states, particularly those of the West African region: Ivory Coast, Benin, Togo, Niger, Upper Volta, Mali, Cameroons and also Gabon, with whom she belongs in OPEC. The intention is not so much to isolate any one reactionary state, but to break and reduce France's stranglehold on her former colonies. The result would not be for Nigeria to boss these States around in the OAU or other international forums but, rather, to enable them to act more independently in the affairs of the continent. Obviously, this requires that Nigeria should respond more sympathetically to the economic problems of these states, at least those among them who most need such response. In this respect, she may not necessarily act alone. She must also encourage other English-speaking states, such as Ghana and Sierra Leone, to cooperate more, economically and socially, with their respective neighbouring states.

Another long-lasting form of cooperation could be in education. Nigeria already has twelve universities and other institutions of higher education. There is no reason why she could not let these universities and institutions serve as centres of learning for students from these neighbouring states, particularly the poorer ones such as Niger, Upper Volta and Mali, and if possible establish exchange programmes through which Nigerian students could study in neighbouring French-speaking universities. It would not be a bad idea if she were even to establish chairs in some of the twelve universities to be held in rotation by scholars from the French-speaking states whose responsibility it would be to bring home to Nigerian students their own thinking concerning common interests within the continent. Needless to say, what applies to her immediate neighbours could be extended to include other states in the continent. In fact, Nigeria could achieve all the above in two ways either directly instituting the programmes herself, or through a special fund established in the OAU. Either way, the end result would be to give the country's universities a continental image.

The final problem I would like to deal with concerns, primarily, Nigeria's own attitudes to the task that is now being demanded of her. Since her independence, Nigeria has suffered from a number of complexes. The first, obviously, has been her size. As I indicated earlier, about one out of every four Africans lives within her borders. This has invariably been seen by many smaller countries, particularly the French-speaking ones, as a threat. France, especially, has for years exploited this fear—if, in fact, she did not herself originally invoke it—to create walls of suspicion between those states and Nigeria. And Nigeria, on her part, has been extraordinarily sensitive and careful not to appear to be the demon she is suspected of representing. In fact, she has been so sensitive and careful of her image in this regard that, at least in her foreign policy, she has often appeared timid and impotent. Fortunately, she rid herself of this unnecessary yoke with her firm and fearless action in the Angolan civil war.

A further complex arose from her own civil war. Since then she has tended to see civil wars elsewhere only in the light of her own experience. Thus she has gradually become a champion of the inviolability of territorial integrity. An example of this was her role in the recent Zairian civil war, in which she acted as a neutral mediator instead of forcefully condemning the interference of France, in particular, but also of Belgium and Morocco. It could be inferred that she played that role only because she did not wish to appear hypocritical.

Another complex may be in the process of revealing itself on account of her new wealth. Only recently, in the quarrel with Senegal over FESTAC, Senghor accused her of throwing her economic weight around. Although Nigeria won out eventually, there is no doubt that she was peeved by the accusation.

Now it should be clear to Nigeria that the leadership mantle, although it may be graciously imposed on her from the outside, has no sweet or smooth paths. If she is going to be able to play the role successfully, she must be prepared to accept a mixture of contrariness: both gentle and firm, sympathetic to others and opinionated about her own interests, sensitive to genuine complaints and insensitive to petty accusations, diplomatic and blunt as the occasion demands. All this will be accepted if, above all, she is seen to place the interests of the continent as a whole above her own.

4 Nigeria and the Liberation of Southern Africa

We have already noted that one of the main aims on which the Organization of African Unity rests as a continental entity, is the liberation of the colonial and white minority oppressed states of Southern Africa. We also noted that this is perhaps the only area in which the Organization can be said to have achieved any measure of success. However, on a more substantial level, this success can be said to be only marginal. There are many reasons for this: a greater part of the failure is, of course, due to the many difficult external factors, but some part of the failure is undoubtedly self-induced. The problems of Southern Africa have been complicated by a number of factors. First, the multiplicity of claims of national and territorial interests made by many countries and regions of the world—from Africa itself, through Europe, and even to the Americas—means that the true interests of those around whom the drama of the region is played are often submerged. A second factor is that Black African States have, for too long, put their trust in the main players in this drama, to the extent of allowing themselves to be reduced to a state of near-impotence.

By referring to 'the main players in this drama', I am not referring to the liberation movements, nor to the Frontline States, nor even to the white minorities of the region. I am referring essentially to those outside powers whose involvement is indispensable to a successful resolution of the problems in

the region, *viz.* the United States, Britain, France, West
Germany and other Western European powers, together with
Japan and, more recently, their surrogates in South America,
i.e., Brazil, Argentina and Chile. It is widely recognised that,
left alone, Southern African whites, in a confrontation with the
Black states of the continent, could not survive. Their resilience
has been due to the support of Western nations, which has, in
essence, been unwavering.

Since the mid-fifties, when the first independent African
states came together to demand political and economic
reforms in the region, their efforts have met with, at best,
hypocritical sympathy from the West. The power of the
Western nations over events in Southern Africa was seen to be
pervasive, since they controlled the economic—and in some
cases even the political—lifelines, both in the white minority
regimes and in the Black African states. Over the years these
Western nations, particularly Britain and France, have exploited their colonial relationship with the African states to
enhance their selfish interests within the white minority states,
especially with regard to South Africa. Not only have they used
the fruits of their economic exploitation of Black Africa as the
source of further investment in South Africa, but they have
called on old political and economic ties to make most of Black
Africa acquiesce in a so-called 'Western solution' to the
problems of Southern Africa. What has brought about the
current change in Western attitudes to the region? As long as
the West was able to enjoy economic and political benefits in
the continent, unquestioned—that is, as long as she was sure of
the servile stance of the Black African states—she would run
with the hare and hunt with the hounds. We begin with
the outright assumption that the present Western attempt to
resolve the Southern African question does not derive from
any sincere humanitarian or moral sense. Rather, it begins with
the assumption that the change in attitude—at least its
outward appearance—is dictated by the new way in which the
West perceives her own interests, not only in the region in
question, but also in the continent as a whole. The West is thus

interested, not only in seeing the issue resolved, but also, and more importantly, in how it is resolved.

Let us consider briefly some of these Western interests, both in the Southern African region itself, and in Black Africa as a whole; that is, to indicate their nature and history over the years, in an attempt to see (1) whether they justify our present optimism in solving the region's problems; (2) why Black Africa has failed to fight against Western interests in the rest of the continent, as a bargaining tool with the West in solving Southern Africa's problems; and (3) what Nigeria, with her growing economic strength, can do to put pressure on those Western nations whose trade and military links with South Africa have grown over the last few years.

I have earlier indicated that one of the major impediments in resolving the Southern African question has been the multiplicity of both internal and external claims. What, especially, are these claims? For Southern African Blacks and for the rest of the Black African states, the question is quite simple: do the subjected Black people of that region have the right to liberate themselves from the shackles of institutionalised racism and colonial oppression forced on them in South Africa, Zimbabwe and Namibia, and until recently, in the Portuguese enclaves of Angola and Mozambique? South Africa's stand is also quite clear and simple. She is determined to protect apartheid, and in order to do so she needs the territories surrounding her—Namibia, Zimbabwe, Angola and Mozambique—as a buffer between herself and the rest of Black Africa. But apartheid is not an end in itself; it is only the means to controlling the wealth of the region, so that the handful of whites in the country can maintain the good life at the expense of the African majority. But she has never formally or publicly acknowledged this claim. She denies the charge of racism; claiming her policy of apartheid is merely a policy of racialism, that is, a policy allowing each race to develop separately according to its inherent capability. She even asserts that the Blacks are in fact happy with the arrangement, and to support this she cites examples of servile Black chiefs and tribal communities who are doing just fine. Having thus established her righteousness, she goes on to claim that those who oppose this system are nothing but Communists who want to take over control of the region for their own selfish ends. This cry against Communism goes beyond the immediate boundaries of South Africa itself. Since her basic argument about her internal policy is difficult to sell, she has had to befog the basic issues involved in the Southern African dilemma in order to win the support of the Western world.

She has done this in two ways. First, she has raised the spectre of Communism in order to alert the ready ear of the Western nations; and, secondly, she has had to try to convince the West that she is not fighting merely for her own selfish interests, but for the larger interests of the Western world: that the West needs her, in fact, more than she needs the West. As for the first, Vorster and the other whites of the region have been eager to explain that whatever atrocities they may have committed have been in order to prevent the advance of Communism in the region. This argument has become more and more appealing and acceptable in the West since the radical transformations which took place in Angola and Mozambique in 1975. The argument goes, that unless the Western World comes to the aid of South Africa to prevent more Angolas and Mozambiques, then Russia and her Communist allies would seize the vital Cape sea route through which passes the bulk of the Middle East oil bound for the United States and Western Europe, and would also control the strategic interests of that area. The measure of confidence with which South Africa supports her claims on the second level is perhaps indicated in a 1975 article published in a government publication, *Scope*, and entitled: 'Why the West needs South Africa'. A few paragraphs from the article will suffice:

Strategically, the sea lanes around the Cape are of tremendous importance to the Western World. About 240 million tons of oil are shipped round the Cape Sea route annually, 90% of which is destined for Europe. Vast quantities of other East/West trade also go round the Cape each year.

. . . For years now, South Africa has been watching with concern, the growing Russian presence in the Indian Ocean and around her Southern Seaway. In the event of a global clash with the West, the communists would regard gaining control of the Cape sea route as a valuable prize. The Communist threat to Africa goes hand in glove with Red Expansionism in the Indian Ocean area. Strategists in Europe and the United States have repeatedly called for joint action to secure the sea lanes of the Indian Ocean and the Cape as they are their main trade lifelines . . .

After noting the several steps being taken by Western nations to neutralise Russian influence, the article concludes cheerily:

Such action by the West is the only way of ensuring that Russia will not obtain a stranglehold on the shipping lanes at the southern tip of the African continent. The security of the Cape sea route and the Southern Atlantic and Indian Oceans are vital not only for the safety of South Africa, but other countries as well. Individual Western nations concerned must make their contribution to safeguarding the sea lanes.

(Quoted in *Africa Report*, Vol. 20, No. 1, January–February 1975)

The interests of Western nations and the extent to which they buy Vorster's argument is also best expressed by Britain's Lord Chalfont in the early part of this year. In an article in which he branded Angola, Mozambique, Guinea, Guinea-Bissau, along with Somalia, Libya, Algeria, Tanzania and Nigeria, as Communists, he warned:

. . . if the mineral resources of Southern Africa or the oil routes around the Cape can be effectively denied to the West, the global balance of military and economic power will have undergone a fundamental and dangerous shift . . . (Taken from an article by Olufemi Omosini, published in *Africa*, No. 67, March 1978)

What is significant about Lord Chalfont's article, of course, is not only that it over-simplifies, but also that it highlights two aspects of Western attempts to resolve the Southern African problem: first, a denial that it is a problem that involves, first and foremost, the interests of Black Africa; and secondly, a tacit assumption that, as Omosini has beautifully put it, the mineral and oil demands of the Western nations are more 'fundamental' than the freedom and just rights of the Black peoples who live in the region. That the West believes in this perverse notion of the events in Southern Africa is indicated by the economic and military relations—despite United Nations pressure to the contrary—that exist between the two countries.

The relationship between South Africa and Western Europe is perhaps more complex and strange than that between it and the United States. Although cultivating very strong economic and military ties with Pretoria, Western Europe has not, unlike the US, written off Africa. Of course, this does not necessarily mean that Western Europe and Japan have a more balanced view of the problems in Southern Africa and the rest of the continent. It is merely indicative of the Western view that, as far as money is concerned, they can have it both ways. And somehow they have succeeded in doing just this.

The British connection with South Africa has been longer and more enduring than that between South Africa and any other country. For decades South Africa has provided for Britain a viable commercial base for British multinationals. In 1974 British investments in South Africa amounted to some $2000 million or 60 per cent of the total foreign investment in that country. (See *Africa*, No. 40, December 1974, p. 25.) In 1976 South African imports of British goods amounted to well over $1.1 billion. Thus, as of 1974, Britain has ranked as the greatest supporter, at least economically, of the Vorster regime. Her military collaboration with South Africa is also extensive. As recently as 1974, a flotilla of the Royal Navy, the largest force to visit South Africa in peacetime, undertook joint manoeuvres with the South African Navy in Simonstown. But Britain has also dominated the economic scene in a number of other African countries. For example, in 1977, Britain's exports to Nigeria alone amounted to about $1.33 billion, exceeding the former's exports to South Africa. Although Black Africa's share of Britain's imports has slipped from 4 per cent to 3 per cent (in 1976), Britain's dominance of economic activities, especially in her former colonial territories, e.g., Nigeria, Kenya, Ghana, Sudan, Sierra Leone, Uganda and Tanzania, is still very strong. Moreover, the figures of 4 per cent and 3 per cent can be deceptive. While in monetary terms the figures seem quite small, in strategic value they are more significant. African exports are a vital raw material which Britain needs in order to operate her factories and, as is already known, this material is under-priced. Again, the decline in British imports does not derive from a decline in her need for it, but is rather the result of great competition from other European nations, particularly West Germany and France, and also Japan.

As mentioned in the introduction, financial experts remarked that Nigeria alone had such great reserves in sterling that, had she decided during the Western economic crisis to convert to some other currency, the British economy would have suffered great damage. In fact, Britain still suspects Nigeria of causing sterling to tumble in 1975 when it was rumoured that she was trying to diversify her reserve currency. All this is to show that Britain's economic interests in Black Africa are still great enough to make her vulnerable, should Black Africa wish to take reprisal measures for her South African policy.

In the last few years France has seriously challenged Britain's dominance of the South African economy. As of 1974, France had gained fifth position, after Britain, the US,

Japan and West Germany, in her economic support of the Vorster régime. In 1973, for example, South African exports to France amounted to R 69.1 million, while imports of French goods were R 125.3 million. These figures exclude military equipment. However, compared with the volume of trade between South Africa and Britain, the French figures are very small. After all is said and done, France still has a much higher volume of trade with her former colonies in Black Africa than she has with Pretoria. It is, in fact, needless to quote figures, because France's political, economic and military domination of these African states is such that it verges on the dictatorial. But France's recently acquired notoriety in her relationship with South Africa has not been based only on economic statistics. It is based on the nature of the cooperation: military. Not only does she supply military equipment, such as Mirage F-1 fighters, helicopters, armoured weapons and submarines, but she has, more than any other nation, perhaps, sold her military technology to the apartheid régime. This is achieved through the manufacture of many of these weapons in South Africa under French licence or through joint efforts in the case of certain advanced weapons. Two examples stand out. A report in the London *Observer* of 1 April 1973 revealed that 'in 1966 when the Wilson government cancelled the agreement to supply Saladin armoured cars to South Africa, France persuaded Germany to build a factory in South Africa so that French armoured cars could be made under licence. The result was that the French landed a lucrative contract without the bad publicity among their Black African customers that direct sales might have caused . . . '. Again, in 1975, another such collaboration was reported between France and South Africa to co-produce ground-to-air Crotale missiles. These are only a few examples.

But how has France been able to engage in such activities with South Africa when, from every indication, her stake in Black Africa, particularly in her former colonies, is so much greater than that in South Africa itself? Why has she, even more than Britain, been able to run with the Black African hare and hunt with the South African hounds for so long unchallenged although her dependence on colonial clients would render her more vulnerable to reprisal than Britain? Why have the Arabs been able to influence French policy towards Israel, while Black Africa has failed to influence France's policies in South Africa, although France has more economic and political stakes in the latter than in the Arab world?

Earlier we noted the peculiar relationships that still exist between so-called 'independent' African states and their former colonisers, that is, the master–servant relationship. This relationship would seem to be responsible for the success of both France and Britain in pursuing policies that supported the Vorster regime, while at the same time exploiting the rest of Black Africa; but more significantly it is responsible for their reluctance, hitherto, to consider Black interests in the Southern African drama as a whole. Both countries, particularly during the heyday of their empires, argued that in exploiting the continent they were in fact doing the Africans a favour by giving them employment and 'the chance to sample the fruits of an all-embracing empire'. In post-independence, the fact that they (in particular France) have been responsible for balancing the budgets of some of the African mini-states gives support to their basic contention. But more cynically, this assertion of doing a favour derives from the old imperial notion that the African is no more than a child who must be guided and told what is good or bad for him. After almost a century of the master–servant relationship, the French and British seem to pride themselves on being the best psychoanalysts of the African mind, assuming automatically a knowledge of what is there without examining it. The sad thing is that they seem to be right. Obviously if, say, France, had suspected for a moment that her African clients might one day hold her accountable for her South African policy, it is a fair assumption that she might have acted differently. But the fact that her insidious relationship with South Africa, even in the face of worldwide condemnation, is tolerated by her Black African clients not only proves to her that she truly knows the African mind, but also encourages her to continue her policies in the belief that Black African interests in the Southern African region are ultimately of little consequence.

Japan and West Germany have equally healthy economic and, in the case of the latter, military links with the apartheid regime in South Africa. In fact, German and French cooperation with South Africa in the development of nuclear technology is chiefly responsible for South Africa's military self-sufficiency. Japan and West Germany were respectively the third and fourth largest trading partners with South Africa, following the UK and the US. To a large extent the pattern of Japanese and American trade relations with Africa are very similar. Both have tended, over a long period of time, to ignore Black Africa, while concentrating on South Africa. During Portuguese rule, Japan also had brisk trade relations with Mozambique and Angola. This indicates the Japanese attitude to the problems of the continent. The desire for a stable atmosphere for her investments has prompted her to choose the racist and fascist regimes of Southern Africa over the rest of Black Africa. She does this under the guise of dissociation from the politics of the continent. Thus, she has become one of the major breakers of sanctions against Rhodesia, and only recently has contracted with South Africa for Namibian uranium, despite the political uncertainties hanging over that territory. It is argued that there is very little that Black Africa can do in this case, since Japan's investment in Africa is a mere 3 per cent of her global total (in 1976) and she has no special colonial ties binding her emotionally to the continent. While this argument is substantially correct, two points need to be made: (1) since 1974 the tempo of Japanese–African trade, particularly with Zambia, Zaire, Nigeria, Liberia and Tanzania, has quickened, and indications are that this trend will continue. In fact, by 1976 her exports to Africa had risen to 8.8 per cent of her global total; (2) Japan is a raw-material-starved country, while Africa—though the least developed of the continents—is the primary source of raw materials for the world. Thus, while she prefers her Latin-American and Asian connections today, she would be foolish to ignore the possibilities for tomorrow, when Africa may loom larger in her consideration than is at present the case.

The relationships between the US and South Africa and the US and Black Africa are, as I have noted earlier, relatively straightforward. For years the US has not only concentrated all her attention on South Africa, both politically and economically, but she has also generally regarded Black Africa (with the exception of Ethiopia, Zaire and Liberia) as being of virtually no value or interest in her global scheme of things. America's attitudes towards Black Africa have been wittily summarised in the South African magazine *To the Point International* (9 February 1976). In the mid-1950s, upon the attainment of independence by an African country, President Eisenhower is reported to have remarked to his Secretary of State, Douglas Dillon: 'Perhaps this day will not even be distinguished by the independence of an additional African State, which will be a great relief, since my mental map of Africa is experiencing great confusion.' In the mid-sixties, the US Ambassador to Zambia, Robert Good, is reported to have said: 'Of all the areas in the world, only Antarctica is less important to America than Africa.' In 1964, President Lyndon B. Johnson is quoted as remarking to British Prime Minister Harold Wilson: 'I keep confusing Nigeria and Algeria because both end in "geria" ', and Secretary of State Henry Kissinger, as replying to an aide who had mentioned President Ngarta Tombalbaye: 'What's Chad?'

America's low regard for Black Africa could be said to have begun with the Eisenhower administration and to have continued through the Kennedy, Johnson, Nixon and Ford administrations. The only time Eisenhower took an interest in the affairs of the continent was in the Congo crisis when America worked to remove President Lumumba from power, because, suspected of Communist leanings, he was thought to be a threat to America's and Western Europe's mineral interests in Katanga. Even his hypocritical criticism of South Africa after the Sharpeville massacre was prompted rather by United Nations pressure than by any moral concern for the deaths of Black South Africans. Kennedy's policy towards Africa was not much more credible. It is true that most Africans will long remember his Peace Corps and even the Kennedy Round, but very few in fact knew or suspected that it was during his administration that South Africa's military technological capability began to expand as a result of cooperative programmes which he initiated with South Africa: (1) space research; (2) nuclear energy research and development; and (3) amendments to the 1954 Atomic Energy Act to permit additional transfers of plutonium to South Africa and Portugal. It was also during his administration that the US began to subsidise South African sugar. President Johnson's only attention to Africa was during Rhodesia's Unilateral Declaration of Independence in 1965, when he had talks with British Prime Minister Harold Wilson. Otherwise, Johnson often regarded African affairs as trivial. This attitude continued through the Nixon–Ford–Kissinger era, culminating in the infamous National Security Council Memo Option Two, which recommended a more flexible US attitude towards white minority regimes in Southern Africa on the assumption that 'the whites are here to stay and the only way that constructive change can come about is through them'.

The Kissinger NSC memo, which was actually written in 1969 at the beginning of the Nixon administration, sought to discourage any kind of confrontation with South Africa; instead, it advocated the so-called policy of communication, encouraging a relaxation of bilateral relations with the apartheid regimes by taking a less doctrinaire approach to 'mutual problems'.

The US and Western Europe's dealings with other colonial territories of the Southern African region have been equally shameful. The fact that, after a period of more than 10 years of supposedly international economic boycott of Zimbabwe (Rhodesia), the Smith regime still survives, is an indication of the US and Western Europe's connivance with South Africa to flout the international community's will. But the most brazen aspect of this connivance was the US contravention of her own freely undertaken obligation under UN general sanctions against the Smith regime; namely, sanctions against the importation of certain Rhodesian strategic and critical materials into the US, including chrome, nickel and asbestos. During the same period, also, the US and her Western allies, under cover of NATO, supplied arms to Portugal, not for the protection, freedom and liberty of Europe, but rather, in the words of Kenya's Foreign Minister, Dr Mungai, 'to obliterate freedom, democracy and human rights in Africa'. Although the US was always aware of Portuguese colonial atrocities against Africans in her territories and even in adjacent independent African states where the politically persecuted sought refuge, she always abstained on resolutions condemning Portugal at the United Nations, just as she, Britain and France have voted against resolutions to apply economic sanctions against South Africa.

But America's attitude towards Black Africa has also been reflected in her economic dealings with the continent *vis-à-vis* South Africa. In fact, it has been generally accepted that America's low regard for Black Africa stems from her marginal economic stakes in the continent. In 1963, according to the UN Economic Commission for Africa, America's direct investments in South Africa alone amounted to nearly half her total investments in all of Black Africa combined. Of these total investments in Black Africa, half were concentrated in only two countries, Libya and Liberia. This meant that, excluding these two countries, American investment in South Africa alone equalled that for the rest of Black Africa put together. Ten years later, by 1973, while American investment in South Africa still remained at nearly 50 per cent of U.S. total investment in all of Black Africa, the amount for South Africa had greatly increased. Thus, for the period 1963–73, America's investments in South Africa grew at the rate of 198.8 per cent, while the rate for Black Africa was 180.5 per cent. Again, this could be deceptive. The increase in investment volume in Africa is attributable mainly to Nigeria's oil, otherwise the volume for all Black Africa would be less than that for South Africa alone by 1973. But whereas the figures may be indicative of the underdeveloped nature of Black Africa's economies, they also reflect America's lack of interest in the continent's development. For instance, the figures show that America's investment in South Africa grew rapidly, because 63 per cent of her earnings were re-invested in the South African economy, while only 29 per cent of earnings were re-invested in Black Africa during the 10-year period 1963–73. Moreover, the situation becomes more outrageous when it is realised that the big volume of earnings in South Africa is attributable to the slave labour of Black South Africans. The rate of re-investment shows that America has deliberately created a situation of strength in the South African economy, with which she goes on to justify the mythical superior ability of the South African white *vis-à-vis* the African, and thereby also justifies the priority consideration that she gives to the apartheid régime within the continent.

All this also accounts for America's foreign policy attitude of indifference to the liberation movements of the Southern African region. It has been suggested that, in order to protect her investments in the region, America has had to be on the side of 'stability' and against 'progressive change'. As we have indicated, America would do so because she had little economic stake in the Black states. As David D. Laitin (*Africa Today*, vol. 23, No. 2, April–June 1976) has remarked:

For many years, American insouciance to the sensitivities of most African leaders cost America very little. All the screaming in the world on the part of the Afro-Asian bloc penetrated American policy makers but little. The President and the State Department could run a coherent foreign policy while totally ignoring the vituperative speeches and statements coming from African States.

THE POSITION SINCE 1975

If America's overall policy towards Black Africa and white-dominated Southern Africa was realistic at the time, it was equally short-sighted, as events have since shown. For America's position has, since the mid-seventies, been eroded on two levels – economic and political. First is the fact that the terms of trade have swung in favour of Black Africa away from South Africa, although this swing is mainly attributed to Nigeria's oil. In 1974 Nigeria accounted for about 46 per cent of total American imports from the entire continent, although American exports still remain insignificant. This increase in American imports increased Black Africa's trade from 3.1 per cent in 1973 to 5.6 per cent in 1974. Since then, it has grown to about 8 per cent, again thanks to Nigeria, Libya and Algeria. By 1976 Nigeria's exports, mainly petroleum and petroleum products, had reached about $2 billion, thus becoming for the first time America's leading trading partner in the continent, far ahead of South Africa. But the increase in the volume of American–Black African trade also goes beyond Nigeria's oil; it could be attributed to the general swing towards commodity producers, e.g., Guinea's bauxite, Zaire's copper, Niger's uranium. This means that Black Africa now has a better bargaining position than she had a few years ago, and withholding her products could have more than a marginal effect on the US consumer. Black Africa's trading position has also improved with respect to Western Europe and Japan since the oil crisis of 1973–74.

The other level on which US ties with Black Africa have undergone tremendous transformation is the political one. This, in fact, has more than one aspect to it. It has been suggested that America's 'neglect' of Black Africa in the 1960s and early 1970s, was due to her single-minded involvement in South-East Asia in order to contain Soviet expansionism. And since 1974, when she more or less disengaged herself from that region after the humiliating events in Vietnam, she has become freer to pay attention to other developing regions. Then there is also the 1974 oil crisis, which convinced the West of the mutual interdependence of nations—the powerful and the weak, the rich and the poor. The crisis, which convinced many third-World nations of their economic power, has also drawn these nations together into a solid bloc, not only in demanding a new international economic order, but also in resolving other global issues, such as the law of the sea. In such a situation, where America's power in the UN has weakened, at least numerically, she can no longer ignore Black Africa, which has the largest single voting bloc in the world body. So not only does Africa possess scarce resources, which the US is less sure of procuring, but Africa also has the votes which the US greatly needs. For the first time, therefore, the relationship between America and Africa has inexorably moved from the level of rhetoric to one in which America sees the relationship as useful to her wider interests.

But all these events do not adequately explain the current increased attention of America to Southern Africa, particularly to its liberation problems, nor her current stand against the *status quo* in the region. The single most significant event which has brought about this change in attitude has been the fall of the Portuguese empire in 1974 and the subsequent Angolan crisis of 1975. There are three aspects of the 1974–75 events which must be considered. First, the collapse of the Portuguese empire meant that the boundary between white-ruled Southern Africa and independent Black African states moved much further south on both the Atlantic and the Indian Ocean sides, giving white minority régimes in South Africa and Zimbabwe a new sense of vulnerability. They were to be flanked by radical and progressive regimes – Zimbabwe, Transvaal and hitherto-enclosed Swaziland by Mozambique, and Namibia by Angola. The unexpected collapse of the Portuguese empire was a jolt to Western countries, especially the United States, which had until that time been the main supporter of the racist and colonial régimes. Secondly, the events gave an impetus to the liberation movements—SWAPO in Namibia and the several movements in Zimbabwe. Guerrilla activities were stepped up, posing further threats to Ian Smith and to South Africa itself, particularly with regard to Namibia. Most significantly, this destroyed the American illusion, as contained in the infamous Kissinger memo, that whites in Southern Africa 'are here to stay' and therefore a change in the region could be brought about only through them.

If these two points reflect only the changed internal dynamics of the Southern African region, the third factor, the Angolan crisis itself, brought in the global element. The victory of the Marxist MPLA of Agostino Neto, through the military aid of Cuba and the political and economic backing especially of Nigeria, and Nigeria's public rebuff of America's pressure on behalf of the Zaire- and Western-supported FNLA of Holden Roberto and the South African supported forces of UNITA, alarmed the United States and her Western allies to the realisation that their one-sided and immoral support of colonial and racist régimes in the region had run its course. Kissinger, whose boss, President Nixon, had some time earlier said that he would visit Africa in 'the next several years', frenziedly undertook an African trip to explain the changed American policy towards not only Black Africa but also the Southern region. In June 1976 in a well-publicised speech in Lusaka, Kissinger maintained that the US stood for ultimate majority rule throughout Southern Africa. This new declaration by the US gave encouragement to Black African leaders that the Southern African problems, particularly with regard to Zimbabwe and Namibia, were at last going to be resolved. Leaders of the Frontline States were prevailed upon by Kissinger to curtail the activities of guerrillas stationed in their territories on the argument that America would use her power to bring about further changes in the region through peaceful means. Kissinger held a series of meetings with these leaders, as well as with Smith and Vorster, by the middle of 1976.

But America and her Western allies had been so long on the side of the oppressors in the region that a good number of thoughtful Africans were cynical about her intentions. How could they believe that America could change overnight to the side of Black Africans? And it was not long before their cynicism proved to be justified. Kissinger, in spite of all his declarations about justice and fairness, had not yet been convinced by recent events to see the problems of Africa in terms of African interests. Rather, to the disappointment of many Africans, he still saw those problems in terms of superpower politics. His primary interest was not to give Africans their due, but to curtail the influence of Russia and Communism in the continent, particularly in the Southern region. America's goodwill towards the continent was, as it were, conditional on the removal of Cuban troops from Angola. Moreover, his approach to the resolution of the problems in Zimbabwe was based on the old assumption, contained in the National Security Council memo, that South Africa holds the key to a successful resolution of the region's problems. He therefore sought Prime Minister Vorster's goodwill in putting pressure on Smith to accept majority rule. Again, many African leaders believed Kissinger might be right in his assumption, since, after Mozambique had closed her border with Rhodesia, Smith had become more and more dependent on South Africa. However, it was not long before Kissinger's true intentions were revealed. In return for Vorster's help in Rhodesia, America would push for only limited reforms in Namibia, while South Africa would be spared any pressure to reform itself. With this, and the increasing intransigence of Smith, the liberation movements and the Frontline States—as well as many other Black African states—finally became convinced that the problems of Zimbabwe and Namibia could be resolved only through increased armed struggle.

THE SOUTH AMERICAN CONNECTION

Another aspect of the South African–Western alliance's desperation over the unfolding events in South Africa is the

South American connection. This connection is developing on two levels: economic and military. The economic link goes back well into the mid-sixties, when South Africa first targeted Paraguay and Uruguay in her drive for South American markets. Both countries established diplomatic ties with South Africa and these ties were strengthened after Vorster visited the countries in August 1976. By 1975 South Africa had offered to grant a R33 million credit to Paraguay to construct two sugar plants and a hydroelectric plant. South African interests also involved mineral exploration, particularly bauxite, and a feasibility study for a fertiliser project. In Uruguay, South Africa agreed to build a cement factory. The South African–Chilean link was initiated immediately after the overthrow of Allende in 1973. Not only did South African investments and manufacturing activities increase rapidly, but Chile is reported to be actively buying arms from South Africa through military missions attached to Western European embassies. Other South American countries developing strong economic links with South Africa are Brazil, Argentina and Venezuela. Thus, by 1974, South African exports and imports, respectively, to and from Latin America were: Brazil R13m/R31m; Venezuela R29m/-; Argentina R3m/R14m; Chile R1m/R9m; the rest of Latin America R18m/R12m (See *New Africa Development*, February 1977).

The result is that, with the collapse of her attempted *détente* with Black African states and her boycott by OAU countries, South Africa has now found willing political allies amongst South America's most repressive dictatorships, and thereby a lucrative market for her products.

The military connection is more cynical. As early as 1969, at the very beginning of the Nixon administration, talks of military cooperation between Brazil, Argentina, Chile and apartheid South Africa, had begun secretly with the quiet connivance of Western (NATO) powers. What quickened the tempo of this alliance, however, was the events in Southern Africa after the collapse of the Portuguese empire and the ascendancy of the MPLA to power in Angola. Nervous of the possible loss of their strategic control over the Cape route, but too embarrassed to establish a direct military link itself with South Africa, the West, led by the United States, sought to encourage these four countries to form an equivalent of NATO on the Southern Atlantic. The purpose of the Southern Atlantic Treaty Organization is threefold: (1) to defend Western economic and strategic interests; (2) to protect the Cape route through which the bulk of Middle East oil passes to the United States and Western Europe; and (3) ultimately to integrate South Africa into the Western defence perimeter. The situation was summed up by Argentina's pro-government newspaper, *La Nacion*, when it wrote:

> Only three countries, who by their culture and their tradition are part of the Western world, have a geographical situation which enables them to play an important role in the control and protection of the Southern Atlantic: Argentina, Brazil and South Africa.

However, these Latin American countries have used Cuban involvement in Angola as a justification for the alliance, which they see as an extension of Latin America's struggle against Cuban 'subversion' in their hemisphere.

The threat of such an alliance is of course already obvious to some Black African leaders of the Southern African region, although surprisingly little is being made of this awareness by the OAU. Nevertheless, the former Angolan Foreign Minister, in a speech at the General Assembly in New York to mark Angola's admission into the world body, declared that the South Atlantic Alliance 'is in effect an offensive military pact against Southern Africa and it constitutes a menace for world peace' (*Africa*, No. 71, July 1977). But what is significant about this, in terms of America's intentions in the South African region, is that at a time when Kissinger was proclaiming American support for majority rule, justice and fair play, and was purporting to be working for peace, stability and harmony in the entire region, he was secretly working to shore up South

Africa economically and militarily through the establishment of trade links with South American countries and the creation of a military alliance which has the encouragement and support of Western powers.

Even closer to home, in the Southern African region itself, other subtle underhand moves of the US were soon revealed. While Kissinger proclaimed America's support for the independence of Namibia from South Africa's illegal control and her acceptance of SWAPO as the legitimate voice of the Black people of the territory, reports revealed that BOSS (the South African intelligence unit) and the CIA were in fact 'marketing' a South-African-supported stooge, Chief Kapuuo, as a more credible Namibian leader. Not only was he being propped up by the two intelligence units and USAID (US Agency for International Development), in addition he was being represented by an American law firm, Burns and Jacoby, in the Turnhalle Constitutional Conference and also by an American public relations firm, Psychographic Communications, which had sent him to the US on a publicity mission, where he had met with key American persons and institutions. This meant that the US and the West were not acting as neutral peace-makers but were determined to settle the Namibian question in their own way, to protect their own economic and political interests. Thus, by the time Kissinger left office, not only had he established a credibility gap for the US, but the whole US diplomatic offensive in Southern Africa had run out of steam.

NEW ELEMENTS IN THE SOUTHERN AFRICAN JIG-SAW

The Carter administration was confronted, right from the start, with very difficult problems in Southern Africa. Some of these, no doubt, were the making of Kissinger and the previous administrations. First of these was overcoming the credibility gap already mentioned. The selection of Andrew Young, former lieutenant to Civil Rights leader Martin Luther King, as America's chief representative at the United Nations, while viewed with some cynicism by a few Black American politicians and leaders as well as by some African diplomats, was nonetheless regarded by most as a positive step in closing that credibility gap. This increasingly became so when he began to emerge as not merely a ceremonial figure at the UN, but rather as one having great influence in the shaping of the emerging American policy towards not only Southern Africa but the continent as a whole. Reflecting the new spirit, Carter's top adviser on foreign affairs, Zbigniew Brzezinski, recently wrote in *Foreign Affairs* (Washington's establishment journal) that:

> Nothing could be more destructive to the United States than to position itself as the ultimate shield of the remnants of white supremacy in Africa . . .

A contrast to Kissinger? The changes which the Carter team seems to be bringing about are: (1) a re-affirmation of American support for majority rule in the region; (2) a recognition of liberation movements in both Zimbabwe and Namibia; (3) a rejection of the Kissinger South African/Rhodesian/Namibian formula, by which South Africa's aid to Rhodesia and some movement in Namibia was to be rewarded with the preservation of the *status quo* in South Africa itself. Instead, the Carter formula encourages America's increased activism, in collaboration with Britain, in the resolution of the Zimbabwe and Namibia questions and increased pressure on South Africa itself for internal change; (4) a declared intention to see the Southern African problems in terms of the interests of Africans themselves rather than seeing them, as in Kissinger's case, only in terms of global East-West superpower strategies; (5) a growing recognition that long-term economic interests in Black Africa are more important than those in South Africa; (6) a beginning to understand the general dynamics of Black Africa's political and social traditions, particularly with regard to the dominant ideologies of capitalism and Communism, and a gradual recognition of

Black Africa's small regard for such imposed ideologies or systems; this would allow for a less visceral reaction to the 'Communist menace' (here, Ambassador Young appears to be a most useful instrument for the Carter administration); (7) as a result of the above, a gradual relaxation of America's customary support for the most conservative, reactionary and oppressive of regimes; and finally, (8) a general recognition of Black Africa's potential and real economic and political power and a desire to court her friendship for genuinely mutual interests. This, in turn, seems to indicate a greater respect for the continent.

Considering America's past record in the continent, as we have earlier noted, and the fact that this administration plunged into the South African political jungle under great suspicion by most Africans, the above changes or trends are no doubt encouraging. Nonetheless, on closer examination, it will be seen that some of Kissinger's legacies still remain intact. For example, while the Carter administration purports to support the liberation struggle in the region, it nevertheless rejects violence, even in the face of Vorster's and Smith's intransigence. Again, in spite of Brzezinski's declaration that America would not position itself as the ultimate shield of the remnants of white supremacy in the region, Carter has yet to disengage Washington and her NATO allies from the insidious Southern Atlantic Treaty Organization, which ties America militarily to South American dictatorships and apartheid South Africa. Lastly, America and her Western allies still reject economic and military sanctions against South Africa, basing this rejection on the spurious argument that such sanctions not only cause Vorster to wax more intransigent but also would hurt only the Blacks.

We have given a brief but general historical survey of the West's, particularly America's (since she is recognised as having the greatest influence in resolving the issues here discussed), relationship with, and attitude towards, Black Africa, South Africa and the general liberation problems of the entire Southern African region. We have not done this merely for its information value, since some of the issues touched upon here are already well known. The purpose has been to examine the history so as to: (1) understand Western attitudes to Black Africa and their sometimes subtle, sometimes crude, connivance at the white racist and colonialist oppression of the majority Africans of the Southern African region; (2) understand the economic and political links between the West and the racist regimes and also Black Africa; (3) better appraise, in the light of the above, the recent change of heart and to see to what extent the present optimism can be justified; and (4) see what areas of vulnerability exist in the Western stance which ultimately, for our larger purpose, Nigeria can use to exert, in her own way, her new economic and political influence to bring about desired Black African goals in the South African region. But, of course, to be able to suggest wisely what Nigeria's course of action could be, we have first to see what the OAU collectively has done, where it has succeeded and where it has failed. This we shall do briefly.

Right from the beginning, when the liberation struggle began in Zimbabwe, Namibia and the former Portuguese empire, Africa has generally followed two paths. Coordinating her strategies through the OAU, she has: (1) worked at the UN to appeal to international conscience so that the world body could understand the injustices perpetrated against Black people in the Southern African region and to bring pressure to bear on Portugal and the white minority regimes to effect a change; (2) given economic, political and military support to the liberation movements and their guerrilla forces, to press the struggle in their respective territories.

As for the first, it is difficult to gauge its success, other than to say that it has won sympathy for the African cause. But the problems of Southern Africa are not the kind that are resolved through mere sympathy. If they were, then they could have been resolved long ago, since in every UN Assembly resolutions have been passed giving overwhelming support to the just struggle of the African peoples and condemning South African/Rhodesian/Portuguese racist and oppressive policies.

Merely reciting such resolutions is thus not useful to our purpose. Let us, rather, indicate briefly Africa's achievement through the UN:

(1) Under African pressure, with support from most of the Third World and, more importantly, the Communist bloc, the UN voted to apply economic sanctions against the Smith regime, when Rhodesia made a unilateral declaration of independence in 1965. This was a great step forward, notwithstanding that many countries (particularly the US) have from time to time violated the UN resolution.

(2) Under pressure from African countries, and with the cooperation of the Asian group, the Communist bloc and a few enlightened Western nations, South African control over Namibia was declared void and illegal. Since then, the UN has tried to establish direct control of the territory with a view to passing that control over to the Namibian people themselves. With South Africa's rejection of the action and her subsequent refusal to abandon control, the UN set up the Namibian Institute in Zambia, which helps to coordinate the UN resolutions as they pertain to the future of the territory.

(3) Under African pressure, the majority of the UN members have refused to have political, economic or military links with Pretoria. The only countries that have rejected a mandatory economic and military embargo against South Africa are the so-called Western democracies: the US, Britain, France, West Germany and Japan, on whom most African countries have generally relied, and the South American dictatorships mentioned earlier.

(4) The UN has generally given succour and aid (though not military) to the liberation movements.

(5) The UN has granted refugees from these territories refugee status, which allows them to travel and have contact with the rest of the world.

(6) The world body has also made financial grants to these refugees to pursue their education, if they so wish, in the outside world.

(7) The International Labour Organisation has generally

given aid to exiled Black labour unions, particularly from South Africa.

Closer to home, at the liberation fronts, more has happened:

(1) The OAU's economic, military and moral support for the liberation movements has had great results. The increased struggle of these movements in the early 1970s led to the most significant event in the entire history of Southern Africa: the collapse of the Portuguese empire in 1974 and the subsequent independence of Mozambique, Angola and Guinea-Bissau.

(2) The changed political and military chemistry of the region has forced the West, particularly the US and Britain, to be more involved in attempts to resolve the problems of the region; the Kissinger shuttle and the present US and British role in Rhodesia, and the 'Contact Group' (Western nations of NATO) pressure on Vorster over Namibia are examples of this.

(3) The OAU support for the Zimbabwe and Namibia guerrilla forces has so strengthened their position that Smith and Vorster have been forced to reckon seriously with them, to the point of giving serious consideration to a re-examination of their apartheid structures.

(4) OAU support has enabled the Frontline States, through their determined support for the liberation movements, to 'put the squeeze' on the minority regimes, particularly in the case of the Smith regime.

(5) Through the OAU in general, and the Frontline States in particular, Western nations have been compelled to bring pressure to bear on Vorster to help to isolate Smith.

(6) The OAU sanctions against South Africa and Rhodesia have been generally successful, except for some violations by a few black-leg states and by a few others whose long historical and economic association with the South African monetary system has made it impossible to break away completely. The OAU has thus created a situation of isolation both for South Africa and Rhodesia, at least in so far as the continent is concerned.

(7) OAU support of the South African liberation move-

ments, both inside and outside that country, combined with the pressure the West has been forced to inflict on Vorster, has helped to create at least the psychology of instability and fear among the Vorster forces.

(8) The tenacity of the OAU, the Frontline States and the liberation movements themselves, have on the whole led to the present feeling of optimism concerning the problems of Southern Africa.

In spite of these commendable efforts, however, there are many areas in which the OAU has been less successful and has at times acted unwisely. Some of these errors no doubt derive from Africa's sense of weakness, especially economic weakness. Nonetheless, sometimes perception of one's own weakness may not reflect one's true stature.

One of the shortcomings of the OAU, as regards the problems of Southern Africa, would seem to have been a basic misunderstanding, even a deliberate misunderstanding, of the true enemy. We have earlier indicated that the white supremacist regimes in the region could never have preserved their apartheid systems for so long, without tacit outside support. Vorster and Smith have understood this and have often stressed the fact that they are members of the Western world and have explained away their racist and inhuman acts as being in defence of Western values and interests. The so-called Western democracies, while they voice their abhorrence of apartheid at the UN, have nonetheless failed to refute the white supremacists' assumption. All their actions, at least until the collapse of the Portuguese empire, have generally tended to support it. We have already cited the economic and military alliance between them and South Africa. It should therefore be undeniably clear that the white supremacists are merely part of a larger evil design. It should be noted that in her application of punitive measures, Africa—that is the OAU—seems to have aimed only at the white leaders of this area. Thus, while they apply economic and political sanctions against South Africa and Rhodesia, African countries have generally coddled those without whom these countries would never have prospered.

Instead, they have shown their anger against these countries only by making noisy speeches at the United Nations, speeches which they hope, nonetheless, would leave their cosy relationships with their patrons intact. And the West, for her part, has generally soothed the African countries with promises of aid.

Another basic reason for this behaviour on the part of the African states would seem to be the assumption that only the West has enough influence to bring about a change in the region, just as Kissinger had assumed that the key to solving the problems lay with the minority whites. Therefore, notwithstanding the West's unconscionable attitude and behaviour, Africa must still pamper and cajole her. But the absurdity of this notion is indicated by the fact that the recent changes in Southern Africa have not been brought about by pleading meekly with the Western democracies but, rather, through the military arms support of the Eastern countries, which, the West tries hard to prove to African states, is essentially for ulterior motives. And, in fact, despite such tangible support, many members of the OAU regard Eastern countries' involvement in the liberation struggles of Southern Africa, and the 'bogey of Communism', rather than Western support of the oppressive white minority régimes, as the real threat to peace and stability in the entire continent.

A further indication of Africa's naive reliance on the good intentions of the West was the abortive so-called Dialogue, through which South Africa sought to gain respectability in the continent without making any changes in the apartheid system. This Dialogue derived from the Nixon–Kissinger policy of 'communication rather than confrontation', although it was clear that the West was not interested in any communication with South Africa which would lead to a change in the apartheid system of that country. What was embarrassing, however, was the enthusiasm with which certain African countries embraced this patent fluke. During this Dialogue period which was being promoted by the Western 'democracies', some of the Frontline States actually clamped down on the liberation movements' guerrilla activities and curtailed their efforts to the point where they were renderd almost impotent. It was only a short while, however, before President Kaunda, one of the exponents of the Dialogue, conceded that he had been 'had'. I make these points, not to denigrate any African leader, but merely to raise the hypothetical question as to whether or not Africa's unswerving reliance on the West has not, in fact, helped to prolong the problems of Southern Africa.

There is yet another area where he OAU has not done enough—the South American connection. One could explain this by claiming that the reason the Organization has not paid much attention to this area is that it does not yet clearly see it as representing a threat to the region. Which would support the conclusion that, in a rather short-sighted way, Africa never concerns itself with a problem until it has assumed irreversible dimensions. Otherwise, should it not by now be clear that if South Africa could find substitute markets and military alliances in the Latin American region, all efforts to effect a fundamental change in the apartheid system would be rendered fruitless? Of course, there are problems involved here. For instance, Black Africa's economic and political ties with South America are rudimentary at best and, as such, they do not give her enough leverage to deal with the latter. However, this type of argument should be seen as simply putting the cart before the horse. Has the OAU made any concerted effort to talk with the Latin Americans, to find out where the problems lie?

A matter of the greatest concern to most Africans has been the white regimes' impunitive military raids into the Frontline States, particularly Mozambique. While the OAU has given economic aid to Mozambique, it has nonetheless remained almost impotent militarily. Of course, this impotence derives from the fact that the OAU has no military command. Yet, would it be unreasonable if the OAU, with the support of Mozambique or other Frontline States being attacked, were to prevail on those African states with stronger armies to come to the aid of a beleaguered nation? Such a step would circumvent the customary reluctance of most strong African countries to be militarily involved in other states, lest they be seen as interfering.

The final point which, to a certain extent, is the most humiliating, is the economic situation in Mozambique and other neighbouring states which, because of a long economic link with South Africa, still allow their citizens to work in South African mines and farms. This economic link not only renders patently absurd the OAU's attempts to isolate and economically strangle South Africa, but it also gives credence to South Africa's argument that Africans who live under apartheid are much better off, economically, than Africans in the rest of the continent. Under these circumstances, how could Vorster take Africans seriously?

Certainly, if Africans took themselves seriously, greater attention would by now have been given to some of these issues. So in the light of the OAU's failure in this respect to date, what can Nigeria do either to galvanise a new OAU effort or to act individually to tackle some of the problems enumerated?

The first thing that Nigeria and the rest of Black Africa must do is to scrutinise more closely the involvement of external powers in the Southern African drama—their ideological and philosophical postures *vis-à-vis* South Africa and Black Africa; their economic and political relationships and their strengths and weaknesses, in order to ascertain where they could be most vulnerable. This should be done with a view to making a scapegoat of one of the Western nations which persistently ignores Black Africa's sentiments with regard to the Southern African issue. France, for example, would be a perfect target. Not only has she been more brazen in cooperating militarily with South Africa (France has been the most adamant among the European Economic Community members in persistently opposing any kind of economic or military sanctions against Pretoria) and in disregarding African objections, but also she is perhaps most vulnerable to any economic reprisal by African states, since her ties to the continent are more pervasive than those of any other Western nation. In his Ibadan University speech (referred to earlier) the Nigerian External Affairs Commissioner, Brigadier Joseph Garba, remarked on this:

> ... But France appears to be making the mistake that Nigeria and Africa will for ever be content with only verbal protests about her active support for and collaboration with the apartheid regime of South Africa. French political insensitivity to the hopes and aspirations of the oppressed people of South Africa cannot continue to be ignored in the name of trade and economic cooperation.

While such sentiments are very welcome, they are long overdue. It is time to move from 'verbal protest' to concrete action. Nigeria cannot keep warning France about economic reprisals while at the same time allowing trade between the two countries to expand at a phenomenal rate. It is time that Nigeria organised a concerted economic reprisal, even on a selective basis, against France throughout the whole continent. It can be expected that French clients in the continent will resist such action, but this should not deter Nigeria and other African countries, whose volume of trade with France is great, from embarking on such tangible action. If we can learn from Franco-Arab relations, it should be clear that most Western nations, particularly France, understand only the language of 'war' and not of 'pleading for understanding'. An economic reprisal against France should send signals also to other Western nations. As Garba has rightly indicated, there comes a time when personal honour is worth much more than trade links, and that time has arrived.

Nigeria and most African states seem to think that quiet diplomacy is an immutable canon of international decorum. But most Africans would agree that the former Nigerian Head of State, Murtala Mohammed, with his open rebuff of US President Ford in the Angolan affair, did more to enhance the African image than did nearly a century of African civility towards Europe. Nigeria could therefore be making a mistake now to rely on guarded displeasure with Western nations who openly collaborate with South Africa. Nigeria has enough economic strength to lead a confrontation with France.

With regard to the South American connection, Nigeria should induce the OAU to make a formal protest to the NATO countries to cut their ties, direct or indirect, with the emerging SATO (South Atlantic Treaty Organization), which is nothing but a lifeline to Pretoria. The OAU should also send formal representation to all relevant Latin American states to seek their support in trying to nip such a nefarious alliance in the bud. Nigeria alone, particularly with her emerging relations with a number of Caribbean and Latin American countries, could also work to bring pressure to bear on friendly states. Nigeria's growing economic relationship with Brazil, allied with the fact that the latter has a large Black population, should facilitate such a diplomatic offensive.

Nearer home, Nigeria should realise that she cannot abandon indefinitely her role in the hot spots of the continent to Cuba. Cuba has done a commendable job in Angola and Mozambique, but it is high time that Nigeria also lent some visible support. For some time it has been rumoured that Nigeria sent troops to Angola during the crisis. But such clandestine support is no longer useful. It is time for Nigeria, when invited, to give her support, militarily or economically, in a more visible manner. Such support, if nothing else, at least has its psychological value. Mozambique and Botswana, where Rhodesian and South African troops carry out their arbitrary raids, should be given priority as recipients of such military aid from Nigeria. If Nigeria cannot work on a direct basis with the country concerned, then let her work through the OAU in legitimising her support.

The final area in which Nigeria's individual support is important concerns the economic reliance of Mozambique and Botswana on South African mines and farms. Nigeria should increase her aid to these states, with a view to breaking the system of contract-labour between these countries and South

Africa. This aid should be targeted specifically to helping the contract-labourers, either by establishing small-scale farming in their own areas or by setting up small-scale industries, or other means of generating jobs within these countries. This would boost their own economy and at the same time starve the South African farms and mines of desperately needed cheap Black labour. Again, such economic ventures could be set up by joint cooperation between Nigeria and the respective government or initiated through the OAU. Either way, the ultimate goal is to break the humiliating economic reliance of these countries on South Africa.

5 Nigeria, Black Africa and the Arabs

The relationship between Black Africa and the Arabs has always been underscored by mutual suspicion. This suspicion is centuries old, dating back to the time when Moslem Arabs organised slave raids into Sub-Saharan Africa and tried to proselytise its people. The present closeness between the two peoples could be said to have its origin in the Pan-African movement of the early and mid-fifties of this century, which sought to fight against European colonialism by forging unity and solidarity among all African peoples, irrespective of differences of race and culture, and by creating an African identity. Curiously, however, one aspect of Pan-Africanism has been the propagation of 'racial supremacy', that is, the supremacy of the African race. What the movement did not explain was how it could forge an ideal of racial supremacy by yoking together two peoples (that is Bantu Africans and Semitic Arabs) who are racially and culturally different.

Obviously, it would be naive to say that the Pan-Africanists were not aware of an inherent absurdity in their philosophy; they were. But they felt that a unity founded on a common African-ness of all the peoples of the continent, no matter what the inherent absurdities, would be more enduring than a unity that stressed racial and cultural differences. It would be pertinent to recall Ali Mazrui's remark about the OAU, that it was based on nothing other than the sentiment that 'we are all Africans'. The Pan-Africanist's error, then, was deliberately to have taken a geographical 'commonness' for a racial and cultural common identity.

The foregoing is not to argue that the Pan-Africanists were misguided. For it is undeniable that the activism and ideas of men like Nkrumah and Nasser, who preached continental unity, have borne visible fruits, the creation of the OAU being but one.

For nearly two decades, Black Africans and Arabs have worked together, whether in the OAU or in the United Nations and its several agencies, in a way that earlier had been thought impossible. Yet, in spite of such commendable cooperation, old suspicions have lingered, although the leaders themselves, finding the subject of Blacks and Arabs too delicate, have generally steered away from open discussion of it. Both sides have tried to give at least a semblance of unity and brotherliness.

African–Arab relations reached a peak in 1973, immediately after the Arab–Israeli war, when, as a result of pressures from the Arab League, nearly all African countries broke relations with Israel to demonstrate their support for the Arab and Palestinian cause. Since then, mutual suspicion has increased, and particularly since the oil crisis, as a result of the quadrupling of oil prices, African leaders have begun to voice openly their reservations about Arab attitudes towards African problems. Most people are now beginning to wonder whether it is not more useful for the two peoples to speak their minds so as to eliminate any illusions concerning their relationship.

The most recent questioning of Afro-Arab ties was made during FESTAC, January 1977, when President Senghor challenged Arab participation in the discussion on Black culture. But the annoyance of many Black leaders over Arab attitudes was perhaps best expressed by Nigeria's Commissioner for External Affairs, Brigadier Joseph Garba, shortly after FESTAC, in his candid speech at Ibadan University on 19 February 1977. His reference to the Black–Arab question was part of a general speech on 'Foreign Policy and the Problems of Economic Development':

Another important point which I would like to raise here is that of Afro-Arab cooperation in all its ramifications. Afro-Arab cooperation in the diplomatic, political, economic and cultural fields increased tremendously after the October 1973 Middle East War when African countries broke diplomatic relations with Israel in support of Arab demands of Israeli evacuation of occupied Arab territories. An identity of views, indeed a perception of a wide community of interests between Africans and Arabs is the driving force behind this increasing Afro-Arab cooperation and solidarity. In two weeks' time, there will be an Afro-Arab summit in Cairo to discuss the various areas of cooperation between African and Arab countries.

Nigeria welcomes this growing cooperation, but such cooperation we believe, must be based on the principle of mutual respect for the sovereign equality of States and for national dignity of individual countries. For us, and indeed for all African countries, the occasional patronising attitude which certain Arab countries have tended to display in the past is completely unacceptable . . .

Brigadier Garba went on to cite two examples of Arab attitudes towards Black African states: (1) in spite of formal invitations and in spite of the trouble Nigeria went through to ensure that they participated, no Arab Head of State (with the exception of the President of Mauritania) attended the Black and African Festival of Arts and Culture in Lagos; (2) no Arab Foreign Minister from the continent attended the first extraordinary Council of Ministers of the OAU held in Kinshasa in December 1976 to discuss problems of inter-African economic cooperation. And he concluded:

If the Arab countries, both African and non-African, want to persuade Black African countries of the genuineness of their solidarity and their sincerity for cooperation then one would expect them to demonstrate this by concrete and positive measures at the forthcoming Cairo summit on Afro-Arab cooperation. Nigeria cannot remain indifferent to the apparent unconcern which many non-African Arab countries seem to be exhibiting towards the problems of Southern Africa . . .

The patronising attitude which Brigadier Garba refers to has a historical background. In the February 1977 issue of *New African Development*, the Sierra-Leonean writer, Joseph Adewole-John, expressed, in more anger and in more detail, African grievances against the Arabs, putting them in historical perspective and also noting in great anguish the position of Blacks in each of the Arab countries. I here quote only two of his points, which I consider more pertinent to our discussion; one political and the other economic:

. . . Pan-Arabism aims to unite the entire Arab world from Morocco, in North Africa, to Iraq, in Asia Minor, and Pan-Africanism aims at the creation of a single African nation and brotherhood.
    To unite the Arab world in effect means to truncate parts of Northern Africa; Libya styles itself the Libyan Arab People's Republic, Egypt was also known as the United Arab Republic, though both are in Africa and are founder members of the OAU. Of the Maghreb countries, only Morocco considers it important enough to include in the preamble to its constitution that Morocco is part of Africa and supports Pan-Africanism; the others are all pledged to Pan-Arabism.

On the economic side, he notes a point that has been most sore to Black African states since the financial crisis which hit the world in 1974 and was partly induced by the quadrupling of oil prices.

Most of the Arab countries accumulated huge surpluses they could not possibly utilize; for most Black African States it was a disaster. Ghana, Ivory Coast, Kenya, Tanzania and Zaire suffered serious balance of payment deficits. The Tanzanian economy was so badly affected that the government had to shelve its five-year development plan. Conscious of the damage done to the Black African economies, the Arab States set up a fund to help countries with the most serious balance of payments problems. But the sum involved was so small that several African countries did not even bother to apply. But perhaps more remarkable was the fact that faced with the problem of handling such huge surpluses, the Arab oil producers turned to American financial institutions to help them re-cycle their petro-dollars. The arrangement was satisfactory to the Arabs; their money was guaranteed and they were relieved of the problem of bad debtors.

Black African countries had their reservations; moving vast sums of money from the Arab world to Western institutions put them at the mercy of those institutions.

Obviously some African leaders are more concerned about the economic issue, just as the Arabs are about the political one. The backroom haggling that preceded the Cairo Summit (the first Afro-Arab summit of its kind) in the early part of 1977, showed this. But the two are so fundamentally intertwined that it would be folly to look at one and not the other. In fact, African leaders who have recognised this are now beginning to be nervous about how much political debt economic cooperation with the Arabs might entail.

It is the contention here that the dreaded political debt is already being incurred, not for the economic aid which the Arab petro-dollar states have given to Black African states, but in the vague anticipation of what the Arabs are likely to give. It is not a debt being paid, consciously, as a result of some *quid pro quo* over a conference table; rather, it is being paid by Black African states in the form of the silence and impotence with which they watch Arab expansionism in the continent in fulfilment of the Pan-Arabic ideal.

It will no doubt be argued that it is unfair to lump all the Arab states together, since (1) there is more divisiveness amongst them than among Black African states; (2) they are not ideologically homogeneous; and finally (3) there are great disparities in the level of wealth, and therefore they cannot all be held responsible for certain Arab League economic policies. While the above is true to a certain extent, it should be stressed that the divisiveness within the Arab world does not derive from any genuine antagonism. Ironically, it derives, rather, from the ferocity and zeal with which they all seek to establish Arab unity, identity and influence. In other words, when it comes to Pan-Arabism, the antagonisms within the Arab world pale into insignificance. And since Pan-Arabism is a living ideology it would not be totally correct to say the Arabs are not ideologically homogeneous. Marxism and capitalism are just as subordinate to Pan-Arabism, at least in its external application, just as these two ideologies would be subordinate to Pan-Africanism if this were a living ideology genuinely embraced throughout the continent today. Moreover, Pan-Arabism, unlike Pan-Africanism, is genuinely racial and culture-derived. As such, it transcends levels of poverty or wealth. Hence, I am convinced that we can talk about the Arab world as a unit.

How is Arab expansionism being carried out within the continent of Africa? Let us go back a few years and begin with Mauritania. Adewole-John has drawn attention to the fact that throughout the colonial era, Black Mauritanians served as the backbone of the civil service when the administrative language was French. On attaining independence the Arab Prime Minister disposed of the French language and made Arabic the language of education. The result was that hundreds of Black Mauritanians were thrown out of their jobs in the civil service and related branches of the administration. Since then the country has been thoroughly Arabised without any consideration whatsoever for the Black population. The Sudanese conflict between the Arab North and the Black South is perhaps more widely known in the continent since it involved a protracted civil war. The civil war was, of course, fought over what has now become an Achilles' heel in most African countries; the domination of one segment of the population over another.

The Southern Sudanese, being Black, had felt that it would be unwise to let themselves be assimilated into the Arab culture of the North. What is disturbing here is not that the majority of the Arab North should want to unite the country at all, but rather, the logic and rationale for their action. The Arabs argued that, since they were in a majority, Arabism should remain the supreme ideology for the North as well as for the South, contending that Arabism was not a racial concept but a linguistic, cultural and non-racial link binding many races together. If this reasoning were accepted at all, it would only mean that Pan-Arabism would do equally well as the supreme ideology for the entire continent. But if this sounds absurd to most Black Africans, it does not at all to the Arabs. How much they believe this is indicated by Libya's unrelenting proselytising missions into Black African states. She has sought to convert Black African states, through their leaders, to the Moslem faith with the lure of petro-dollars. But Libya's most brazen act in this direction so far has been her forcible occupation of the northern parts of the Republic of Chad. Yet, in spite of all these affronts, most Black African leaders still put on an air of serenity in the grand halls of the OAU, as though nothing is actually happening. Chad has cried out so much in vain that she has been compelled to call on France to rally to her support and defence.

Absurd as this may sound, there is a strong indication that the single most potent instrument of Arab expansionism in the continent is the Organization of African Unity. How does this work? It has been remarked by many that the only Arab interest in the OAU is to use it to promote the interests of the Arab League—the forced break-up of relations between Black states and Israel in support of the Palestinian cause is a case in point—when necessary, and to ignore it when they do not find its deliberations worthwhile. The two examples cited by Brigadier Garba earlier support this contention. Another example was the Arab response to the events in Zaire, when Katangese rebels based in Angola (these rebels had fought with the Portuguese fascist forces against the forces of the Neto Government) invaded their own country in an attempt to force out Mobutu. The catalogue of Arab forces that came to Mobutu's aid—Morocco, Egypt and Syria and Saudi Arabia, with her petro-dollars—is less significant on reflection, than the argument put forward for their action. It is well known that Saudi Arabia has a great dislike for the emerging radical States and liberation movements in Africa. So her desire to see the radical government of Angola overthrown, since President Neto made it clear that the introduction of foreign arms into Zaire was a threat to her government, could be well understood. But the rationale put forward by Morocco, Egypt and Syria was that a threat to the government of Mobutu was a threat to the Sudan. In other words, their interest in intervening in Zaire was not so much the preservation of Zaire's territorial integrity as to safeguard Arab Sudan.

Thus, if the OAU is the most potent single instrument of the propagation of Pan-Arabism, the most valuable article of that instrument is the do-or-die defence of Territorial Integrity and the Inviolability of National Boundaries. Black African states stood aloof from the civil war in the Sudan because of their great respect for that Article of the OAU charter. They also stand aloof from Chad because Gadafi regards his war with that country as an internal matter. If this sounds illogical then the question must be asked: why is it that the Arab States have not come to the aid of Chad in her war with Libya, since Chad's boundary with the Sudan is longer than that of Zaire. Is it because Libya is less radical than Angola and therefore of less threat to the Sudan?

But it will be seen that the Arab members of the OAU have always viewed the sovereignty of states and the inviolability of national boundaries with a double standard. When the Article of the charter conflicts with their interests, they show very little regard for it.

The clearest instance of this is what is presently happening in the Horn of Africa, where Ethiopia is virtually besieged on all sides by Arab states. It should be noted that the secessionist province of Eritrea has waged its war against the government in Addis Ababa for so long only because the province is encouraged, funded and militarily equipped by the non-African States of Saudi Arabia and Kuwait and other States around the Red Sea. These states have also funded and equipped the Sudan to fight Ethiopia from the North-West and have encouraged and supported Somalia to attack from the South-East in order to put the squeeze on the sovereign state of Ethiopia. Moreover, the Sudan and Somalia have made their states free territories for the anti-Ethiopian forces whose only aim seems to be the restoration to power of the royalist and conservative elements who had worked with Haile Selassie to oppress and dehumanise the Ethiopian masses. However, if the aim of the Ethiopian rebels is purely nationalistic, the aim of their Arab patrons is indeed very different. Their aim is to create a unified Arab zone along both sides of the Red Sea and right down to heart of Black Africa. And those who may see this as mere hysteria have only to look further to the case of the recently independent State of Djibouti. Although the enclave population is fairly divided between Blacks and Arabs, a few days after the independence ceremonies ended, the Arab leader declared the country an Arab state and immediately applied for membership to the Arab League. The League's response to the Djibouti application was further proof of Arab intentions in that part of the continent. Although the little enclave and the Comoro Islands made applications for membership to the League at the same time, and although both states use French, and not Arabic, as the official language, the Comoro application was deferred indefinitely while favourable consideration was given to Djibouti's request because of its strategic location on the Red Sea. What is puzzling is that, throughout all these provocations against Ethiopia, the only non-Arab state in the area, no Black African state has cried 'foul', pointing out that a basic principle of the OAU charter is being trampled upon.

These disturbing events around the Horn and the Red Sea and the recent transformation of the Sudan into a bulwark of Pan-Arabism lead us to another question that goes beyond African-Arab relations in the region. It involves the curious relationship between the United States and Western Europe on the one hand and the Arab states, spearheaded by Saudi Arabia and Egypt, on the other. Here, the two blocks argue that they have common interests in seeing to the security of the region: both are concerned with the safety of the oil region, so what is good for the Arab oil states is good for the Western consumers; the Arabs are scared of the incubus of communism infiltrating North-East Africa, the West is also only too happy to reduce the influence of Russia in the continent. The result is that with the encouragement of the Arabs, the United States, which had hitherto been aloof from the continent (except in Selassie's Ethiopia and Mobutu's Zaire), is now suddenly building up clients in the North-Eastern region at a time when Africa is trying to reduce outside influence and interference in her affairs. This developing trend has been summed up in a recent article, written by Flora Lewis, entitled 'African Power Vacuum Draws Outsiders into Struggle for Influence', with a sub-heading 'French Adopt Strategy Aimed at Entire Continent' (*International Herald Tribune*, 2 August 1977):

France has evolved a broad African policy that has as its long-term goal the extension of France's special relationship with its former African colonies to each of the countries of the continent . . .

France's strictly limited, but successful, recent military interventions in Zaire and Chad, in which it provided transport and support for African forces, were an example of the more active interest Paris is taking in African affairs . . . President Valéry Giscard d'Estaing, who is jokingly said to tell officials at his Elysée Palace to 'think African' has consciously extended French interests first to

French-speaking countries that are not former colonies, notably Zaire, then to former Portuguese territories, and now to all African states.

So far, at least, French African policy is not seen as competitive with those of the United States or Britain, but rather complementary . . .

US officials, although discreet in public, have welcomed French initiatives. Among US diplomats, France is now called 'our best ally outside of Europe'.

The ideas behind the general policy, as a high French official described them, are quite simple, although the application is much more complicated. They stem from a basic long-term view: France is dependent on imports for the bulk of its fuel supplies, including both oil and uranium, and Africa is a convenient source . . .

Paris feels that African-Arab relations will continue to have important implications for Europe. For example, Saudi Arabia's growing interest in the Horn of Africa could help to maintain the independence of Djibouti, the last French colony to gain independence, and helps France develop closer relations with the Saudis.

. . . The French seem to believe in a 'domino theory' for Africa, and their major fear after the Angolan civil war was that friendly governments such as those of Senegal and Ivory Coast, would feel endangered to the point of drifting toward a pro-Soviet orientation. Therefore French aid is carefully selective, following Mr d'Estaing's guideline of 'help for friends first'.

In a fascinating conclusion, the article reports that the French, in their conviction that the African is no more than a child who needs to be guided through his development, believe that:

By long tradition and cultural history, Africa is uncomfortable in what an official called the 'Capitalist jungle'. But as soon as theoretically appealing socialist approaches are translated into the mobilization of political and economic forces, the Africans become even more ill at ease. The Africans in general, Paris thinks, are looking for a 'third way', and it is up to France and the West in general to help them create a structure to support a new alternative.

But the French feel that there is, as yet, no underlying structure in Africa. All it has for dealing with the world is the State system left behind by the colonial period. Without that system, there would be general chaos. Therefore, the French say, the territorial integrity of existing states, proclaimed by the Organization of African Unity, must be supported with every possible effort.

Before one can take an overview of the French thinking, one question is urgently pertinent: If the territorial integrity of existing states, proclaimed by the OAU, must be supported with 'every possible effort', then why does the West support Saudi Arabia, Somalia, the Sudan and the Eritrean rebels whose aim is to forcibly change the territorial boundaries of Ethiopia? Or Zaire and South Africa, who are determined to see that the province of Cabinda is broken away from the Sovereign State of Angola? Or France, in particular, who during the Nigerian Civil War was determined to see Nigeria balkanised? But there are other significant points raised in the French view of Africa. The first is that the West has abandoned its subtle attempts at recolonisation of the continent in favour of bold and open methods. Secondly, this process will be made possible through collaboration between the West and the Arabs. And thirdly, the instrument for this recolonisation is the OAU.

Again, as the French view has stressed, the aspiration for the political domination of the continent is rooted in the West's economic needs. Thus we come to the other sore point in African-Arab relations.

We have indicated earlier that the economic issue seems to be of more concern to Black African leaders in their efforts at cooperation with the Arabs. The main points of grievance have already been noted by both Brigadier Garba and Adewole-John. But a few of these points need amplification. First of all, a basic Black African complaint has been that the oil-rich Arab states have not been doing enough to help Black African states to solve their economic problems, which were aggravated by OPEC's quadrupling of oil prices after the Arab–Israeli war, and that the Arab states, instead of shifting their petro-dollar surplus to where developing states could borrow at favourable terms, are placing their money in Western banks and institutions, with the result that Black Africans, who constitute the world's poorest states, are put at the mercy of those institutions. Furthermore, Black African states, along with the rest of the Third World, have been asking OPEC for concessionary oil prices as the best way to alleviate their problems. OPEC, not wishing to create a two-tier system, has rejected this and has instead insisted that the Organization's increased contributions to world financial institutions should be enough to offset the most serious financial problems of the poor countries. The question which bothered the Third-World states, of course, was what the extent of aid to the institutions would be.

In 1973 the total OPEC aid commitments stood at $3 billion. In 1974, however, these rose to $16 billion. Disbursements within the same period also rose from $1 billion in 1973 to $5 billion in 1974. In 1975 total OPEC aid figures represented 3 per cent of members's GNP and 10 per cent of the current balance-of-payments surplus. And by 1976 OPEC's aid of all kinds had risen to 8 per cent of GNP. While these figures undoubtedly look impressive, it is to be noted that very little of it ever flowed into the coffers of Black Africa.

Perhaps there is the easy temptation to regard OPEC and the Arab States as being synonymous, because the latter dominate the former. Most of the Arab oil states, outside the umbrella of OPEC, have individually and through the Arab League itself established various funds whose aims are to help developing countries and specifically the Black African states. The Arab Summit in Algeria in 1973, for instance, established three organs through which such funds are to be disbursed. The Arab Fund, which provides loans to help with the price of oil; the Arab Bank for Economic Development in Africa; and the Arab Fund for Technical Aid to Africa. In 1974, again, another fund, the Arab-African fund, was created. On the face of it, at least, these funds would indicate a certain generosity on the part of the Arabs and especially so as the percentage of total GNP which the Arabs devote to aid to Black Africa and the rest of the Third World is many times that given by the industrialised members of OECD. But let us see how the funds of the Arab institutions geared to helping Black Africa have been disbursed.

Between November 1973, when the fund was set up, and April 1975, the Arab Bank for Economic Development in Africa had made 18 loans to 18 Black African states, totalling $124.5 million. In 1976 the Bank made a further three loans to three African states, amounting to a further $143 million. After much pressure by African states at the 1977 Afro-Arab Summit in Cairo, the Arabs again boosted their pledges to a record $2.2 billion, with Egypt offering $1 million, Saudi Arabia $1 billion, Kuwait $240 million, Qatar $76 million, and United Emirates a further $123 million. The question is, then, with all these pledges, why do Black African states still complain about the Arabs?

First of all, the monies indicated above are only pledges, not hard cash. Secondly, African states still consider the level of aid low in the light of Arab surpluses and in the light of the fact that it is less than the withdrawn Israeli aid to Africa. Also painful is the fact that the Arabs made a loan to Pakistan, a Moslem state, to the tune of $1.7 billion, just for arms—an amount many times that given to all Black African states put together. Thirdly, the destination of the money voted by the Arabs is never precisely known. This worry is real, since the Arabs have tended to pay more attention to states of the Moslem faith. Fourthly, the Arabs have resisted channelling their aid through the African Development Bank; rather, they have insisted on operating through institutions which they control. Fifthly, the

Arab loan rates are high, compared with those of other international institutions. All these complaints are undoubtedly genuine, especially in the light of the political price that the Arabs demand from African states.

It would be unfair, however, to say that the Arabs are completely impervious to the economic worries of Black African states, or to make scapegoats of them for the economic woes of the continent. There are dangers in the African attitude, which, firstly, tends to suppose that the Arab states are already developed and do not have economic problems of their own: Second, as Guy Arnold has pointed out (*New African Development*, February 1977):

> . . . the aid relationship between rich and poor has long been highly dangerous to the poor because whatever short-term relief particular aid may bring in the long run the resulting indebtedness simply deprives the recipients of room in which to manoeuvre or develop as they would wish. The danger in the current growing African dependence upon Arab aid is the same precisely . . .

Perhaps the Chairman of the Arab Bank for African Development, Chedli Ayari, put it more precisely in the same issue of *New African Development*:

> We must avoid oil aid or drought aid. The psychology of emergency assistance entails a danger; it represents gifts that fail to serve the future.

This warning points to a third danger which, in some respects, is the greatest of all. The psychosis of dependence prevents the Black African aid recipients from developing an objective overview of the kind of economic cooperation they seek with the Arabs. It destroys foresight in exchange for quick, short-term advantages.

What is this objective overview? First, the oil wealth of the Arabs has made them competitive partners in a number of world financial institutions. And as the financial balance tilts in favour of the Arabs, the Middle East has gradually become a world financial centre of its own. Therefore, the Black African states will, from now on, have two financial centres to confront. Economic power brings political power and it would be naive on the part of Black African states to think that the Arabs with their newly acquired status will be any different from their Western industrialised counterparts. That the Arabs will utilise their new status as befits a financial superpower is already indicated by their new political activism in the eastern region of Africa and the new alliance that they are forging with the West in that and other areas of the continent. A major question confronting Black African states, then, is how to meet the new challenge of two competing economic superpowers, instead of seeking economic cooperation that puts the poor entirely on the sufferance of the rich.

Admittedly the economic aspect of the Afro-Arab cooperation is more difficult to deal with than the political one, and I do not pretend to have the answers. Yet certain points may indicate the extent of the problem. For instance, can the Black African states demand and obtain from the Arabs an economic cooperation based on: (1) equality of the states; (2) mere friendliness as a result of geographical proximity; (3) economic aid in exchange for political concessions, or an economic *quid pro quo*? What do Black African states have, in the area of trade, which they can use as bargaining chips with the petro-dollar Arab states; that is, what commodities can they offer the Arabs in bilateral economic cooperation? This last point has already been stressed by some African economists, who have suggested that the new economic re-alignment would require a concomitant re-alignment of the trading patterns between the rich and the poor. They argue that a realistic approach to any economic cooperation between Third-World countries and OPEC (in this case, between Black African states and the Arabs) would be to encourage the exportation of raw materials to the oil-producing countries of the Middle East, away from traditional European markets, possibly through the creation of economic blocs like ECOWAS, the now defunct East African Community and the Union Douanière d'États de l'Afrique Centrale (UDEAC). This would involve the exportation to, say, Saudi-Arabia, of such items as fruit and vegetable products, forest products—timber and timber products (plywood, etc.) for the building industries in the Middle East, which Black Africa has in abundance, or even light manufactured goods from such countries as Nigeria, Kenya, and Ivory Coast. The absurdity of the present economic link—if it can be called a link—between Black African and Arab oil states, was summed up by President Kaunda of Zambia at the Cairo Afro-Arab summit:

> Zambia still buys Saudi Arabian oil from New York and Arab States still buy African tobacco, tea and copper products from European markets.

But the views of President Kaunda, although pointing in a positive direction, have their limitations. For instance, shifting raw materials away from their traditional European markets presupposes that the Arab oil states already have the capacity to absorb such exports. But this is not the case. The Arabs, as developing countries like the rest of the Third World, just do not have the necessary infrastructure to justify such redirection of trade. Again, Kaunda's suggestion presupposes that the Arabs and the Africans have total control over the direction of their exports. To have such control will require a thorough overhauling of these countries' economic structures and their relationships with the industrialised world so that foreign companies operating within their borders are made responsible to those countries rather than to the headquarters in the industrialised nations. But these changes, while desirable, will take time to be realised.

Moreover, although both groups have common problems of underdevelopment and a common desire to industrialise, it would be naive to think that these interests are going to be realised through common strategies. Although not voiced openly, it can be seen from the Arab world's reluctance to discuss economic issues at the Cairo Summit that they do not see the advantage of casting their lot with a world that has very little to offer them, in regard to realising their industrialisation goals. Nor should this be a surprise. Long ago, in 1960, writing in *Fraternité* (February 1960) President Houphouet-Boigny of Ivory Coast voiced the hidden sentiments of most developing countries when he rejected solidarity with the so-called Third World because they 'cannot, given their present state of affairs, offer us anything other than the sharing of their own poverty'. It would therefore not be far-fetched to assume that the Arabs also would operate on this rationale. Lastly, there is what Samir Amin has referred to as 'the essential condition for cooperation: real equality between partners' (*Neo-colonialism in West Africa*, New York: Monthly Review Press, 1973). Would the Arab oil superpowers see themselves as equal partners with the poor Black African states in any Afro-Arab economic cooperation?

But does this mean that any talk of economic cooperation between Black Africa and the Arab world is irrelevant? Not necessarily. The issues raised here are meant to accomplish at least three things: first, to kindle awareness of the principal problems involved; second, to allow a more objective approach to these problems in the development of economic cooperation between Black Africa and the Arab world; third, to draw attention to the natural resources of Black Africa, which could provide a bargaining leverage in any such cooperation, rather than to view any cooperation as perpetuating a dependency psychosis, as has been indicated earlier. Cooperation of this order would demand that Black African states barter away their political rights also.

Until all these problems are resolved, what kind of economic cooperation is possible between Black Africa and the Arab world? For cooperate they must, particularly in an evolving world of interdependence.

Any genuine cooperation will have to take the following points into consideration. First, the shifting of Black Africa's raw material exports away from traditional European markets to the Arab world, while it has its limitations, could nonetheless be encouraged—although it must be according to the pace of absorption of such materials by the Arab countries' economic infrastructure. Second, while the provision of aid by the oil-producing Arab states would be welcomed, efforts should be made by Black African states to go beyond this and the redirection of exports, so as to concentrate on making their countries attractive outlets for the investment resources of the Arab oil-exporting States. As Professor Adediji, the executive secretary of the Economic Commission for Africa (ECA), has pointed out in *Africa—International Perspective* (December 1975/January 1976, p. 13), this might help the countries that benefit from such investments to import more capital goods from developed countries for their own development. In fact, Adediji has noted that the central problem in the strengthening of economic cooperation among developing countries is 'how best to secure a substantial increase in the flow of financial resources from capital-surplus to capital-deficit developing countries'. Such investment in African countries would also help these countries to break the stranglehold of 'the transnational corporations of developed countries', not only as regards financing but also 'in terms of the basic investment strategy to be followed' by the African countries.

However, Black African states should not have any illusions that the kind of economic cooperation with Arabs suggested here will be easy to achieve, particularly in the present political situation in this region of the world. The situation is even further complicated, since, as argued earlier, Black African states have to deal with the Arab financial centre as well as that of the West. This means that cooperation with the Arabs requires a well-planned, well-coordinated strategy. We are already aware of the fact that, no matter what the extent of their cooperation with the Arab world, Black African states would still, for a long time to come, rely on European markets for their industrialisation programmes.

Such a strategy would require the solidarity of Black African states, at least on an economic level, as an essential pre-requisite. And here the importance of regional economic blocs cannot be over-emphasised. But for such regional blocs to be effective (that is, so that different regional blocs in the continent do not destroy each other in seeking advantages from any of the two economic superpowers), some articles of understanding between them will be necessary, and such articles could be lodged with the OAU Economic Cooperation Committee, a body responsible for monitoring regional cooperation. It would also be necessary for all present regional groupings based solely on linguistic and past colonial identity to be dissolved. In fact, it had been hoped that the bringing together of the former Monrovia and Casablanca blocs of African States would accomplish precisely this. This would also eliminate the signing of preferential trade agreements between individual members, which work against the solidarity of the regional bloc itself. A simple example can be taken from the European Economic Community. Any African country dealing with the EEC knows that it is dealing with the whole of Western Europe. On the other hand, the EEC likes to deal with African countries on an individual basis. African countries must learn the lesson of presenting a united front. Thus, the new regional blocs would have two main advantages: (1) Solidarity among the partners would ensure common trade policies and prevent bilateral agreements between any one of its members and either of the two economic superpowers. This would strengthen the competitive power of those states against either of the two dominant world economic blocs. (2) Such an African regional bloc could also aim at destroying or preventing any unity, real or perceived, between the two financial blocs that works against the interests of Black Africa.

Let me immediately clarify what I mean by destroying or preventing the unity of the two blocs. Certainly it does not imply any nefarious acts against either of them. But it should be remembered that there is great temptation for the Arab oil states to invest their surpluses in the West, rather than in Black Africa. And the determination of the West to be the sole repository of those surpluses is even greater. The Arabs would see the advantages of (1) safety for their money; and (2) a bargaining leverage in the resolution of Middle-East problems. On the other hand, the West will stress (a) the advantage of (1) to the Arabs; and (b) the resolution of the Middle-East problems as a trade-off for the Arabs in keeping their money in the financial centres of New York, London and Paris. Finally, the West's involvement in the Horn of Africa should not be seen only as an attempt to prevent Communism. It should be seen also as an attempt to ingratiate themselves with the Arabs so as to increase the economic cooperation between the two, as the French have already indicated, and at the same time to minimise such cooperation between the Arabs and Black Africa. For a direct economic link between these two is not in the best interests of the former, since it would weaken her control over both.

It would, of course, be in the best interests of Black African states to subvert such a strategy. One way of doing this would be to stress to the Arabs that, while they are not being asked to abandon cooperation with the West, it would be in their interest to develop a closer economic link with the Black African states, as a kind of counter-weight to the dominance of Western trans-national corporations. Moreover, the Arabs must be made to understand that, while their efforts to industrialise are commendable, ultimately this will lead to a greater demand for raw materials. This would indicate that, to a large extent, the future success of their industrialisation programmes lies in the hands of Black Africa and her raw materials. There are indications that the Arabs are in fact aware of this state of affairs. Their enthusiasm in luring the Sudan into the Arab fold, making her into a granary for the Arab world, is undoubtedly a well-calculated strategy. But the Sudan alone cannot satisfy all their future raw material requirements. The African states, therefore, while moving into industrialisation themselves, should not ignore the potential of their raw material wealth.

Words alone of course will not convince the Arabs to invest

more in the continent. The Black African states must create an atmosphere of security, as Adediji has suggested. Furthermore, the strategy so far indicated would require that the regional blocs mentioned earlier, rather than evolving a uniform trade policy towards the West and the Arabs, could instead adopt policies that are more advantageous to the Arab bloc than to the West, say, regarding those commodities in which the Arabs show more interest and in which they are in great competition with the Western or Eastern consumers.

It would, of course, be argued that Black Africa has more to gain from the West than from the Arabs, particularly in the area of economic and technical aid, or even that Black African states, being so poor, cannot take an economic offensive against the rich states of the world. While these two arguments no doubt have some truth in them, four points should nonetheless be taken into consideration:

(1) Black African states cannot for ever depend on Western aid. Not only is the present level of economic aid too low to help industrialisation (nor is this a desired objective of industrialised states), but it has the disadvantage of perpetuating a dependency psychology.

(2) In over a century of close economic cooperation with the West, Black Africa has never enjoyed an advantage or concession, even by adopting policies that give commodity preferences to Western markets. In other words, the West has been trying and has failed. An offensive against it, therefore, would anticipate no worse results. (See Samir Amin in *Africa— International Perspective*, December 1975/January 1976, pp. 35–36, where he argues that in over 150 years of cooperation between the West and Africa, the latter's standard of living has remained below 5 per cent of that of Western capitalist–industrialised countries).

(3) The industrialised West has in any case, for centuries, practised the policy of fragmentation, or 'divide and rule', against African States.

(4) The Arabs are a new bloc, and it would not hurt if Black African states tried to seduce them with trade policies which

could draw both groups closer. Even if such policies failed they would not have worse results than Black Africa has realised from the West.

The question may be asked whether it is possible for Black African states to adopt a policy of confrontation with the Arabs on the political level and a policy of cooperation on the economic level? Is it even realistic? Admittedly, it will not be easy. Some political re-alignment in the continent may even be required. However, what we are advocating is not the erection of a Sahara wall between Black Africa and the Arabs, but rather, the creation of a situation whereby cooperation between them is seen more objectively, so as to eliminate misconceptions and illusions. If such misconceptions and illusions can be removed, and if mutual respect and equality between the two blocs could be established, and if both blocs have the desire, then there is no reason why cooperation on both the economic and political levels should not be realised; such cooperation would be to the benefit of all.

This brings us to the question which has been our major concern: What can Nigeria do, as the leader of Black Africa, to realise the changes we have thus advocated?

Nigeria is in a particularly strange situation here. So strange that to some extent she could almost be said to fall into the same situation *vis-à-vis* the OAU as most of the Afro-Arab states. Her present leadership role is very much dependent on her economic strength. Yet her economic strength derives from her membership of OPEC, the same Organization which has made the present economic status of the Arabs possible. How, therefore, can she politically confront those states which constitute the majority in that Organization which is the very source of her wealth? Although this factor cannot be ignored, it would be wrong for Nigeria to allow her policies towards the continent, and particularly towards the Arab states, to be excessively conditioned by it. If she does this, she will not only betray the 'greater interests of Africa' but she will weaken herself to the extent that her capability to take a leadership role in the continent would be questioned. So what can she do?

On the political level, there are a few points which should be noted in addition to those already indicated, which it may be in her interests to examine carefully. First, if the OAU is to remain in its present geographical composition, then it may be useful for her to work to revise the Charter so as to (a) strengthen its enforcement or mediatory mechanisms with regard to intra-national disputes, possibly through the creation of an OAU Military Command, so that only such a Command would be empowered to intervene militarily in such disputes; (b) specifically bar military intervention in such disputes by any outside foreign power and any such foreign intervention, whether at the invitation of any client state or not, would be regarded as an attack against the OAU itself; (c) bar membership of two political blocs whose interests and philosophies are irreconcilable, at least as far as the 'greater interests of Africa' are concerned. On the other hand, as a more drastic measure, the OAU could be allowed to die a natural death so that out of it, like the proverbial phoenix, could arise a less unwieldy organisation, based not on geographical affinity, but on mutual economic and political interests. Such a new entity would obviously have to embrace only those Black states of the continent whose first loyalty is not to the Arab League. It should then be easier for such a new organisation to deal with the Arab world on a bloc-to-bloc basis, just as either bloc would deal with, say, the European Community.

This should not destroy economic cooperation between the new entity and the Arab world. Such cooperation could still be possible, particularly if it is stressed that it is not only in the interests of Black Africa but also of the Arab world; that in a fast-changing world the Houphouet-Boigny dictum may have lost its relevance or truthfulness; that, in fact, economic solidarity amongst the developing states may in the long run be the only hope of the developing world—states with surpluses and those with deficits alike.

6 Africa and the International Organisations

Many Third World nations, having gained independence, find that they are still bound to positions of economic dependence upon their colonial masters, the industrialised world. For many years, however, it was assumed that all that they needed to get out of their position of dependence was some aid and technical assistance from their rich neighbours. At first, such aid and assistance was thought best channelled directly between the 'generous' industrialised country and the poor recipient. Over time, however, as a result of the conditions laid down by the donor country the poor recipient deteriorated from a position of simply being needy to that of being a mendicant. Finally, the poor countries realised that it would be better for help to be channelled through the several agencies of the United Nations, rather than directly between one government and another.

However, while this was good for the self-respect of the poor recipients, channelling aid through some amorphous agency robbed the donor countries of the feeling of being virtuous, since their names could no longer be directly associated with such aid. It is not surprising, then, that the amount of aid and assistance given over the last few years has gradually dwindled, despite the proclaimed desire of the donor countries to make the last decade a decade of development and progress for the poor nations. All has happened is that the dependent countries have become poorer and more dependent while the richer countries have grown richer. And the poor nations have belatedly realised that their problems cannot be solved through a pittance donated by the richer ones.

The current demand for a new international economic order is therefore welcome and long overdue. But while there is some optimism that a new economic order might provide a cure for the ills of the poor countries, it is curious that the vehicle through which new development strategies might be carried out, the United Nations system, seems to have received comparatively little attention. For example, why has the United Nations, through its several agencies, not successfully carried out the programme for the First Development Decade? And how is the UN system to be affected by the new economic order? What is sad is that most of the newer independent countries, the majority of which are in Africa, seem not to understand how the system's several agencies work, even when the agencies are supposedly helping them to carry out their national development plans. I intend here to examine briefly the relationship between African countries and some of the United Nations agencies and affiliates.

Something that is not often stressed, if realised at all, in the relationship between African (as well as most other developing) countries and the United Nations is their conflicting objectives or, rather, the conflict between what the Organisation is supposed to do and what the new developing countries expect it to be doing. This conflict is not something deliberately created; it derives from the origin of the Organisation itself. When the United Nations was first created in 1948 immediately after the Second World War it was a rich man's club and its main objective was to solve the problems of the rich nations, particularly Western Europe, which had been devastated by war. At that time, most of the world's population lived under the suzerainty of some of these rich nations. Most of the so-called Third World, as we know it today, did not exist. Therefore in the creation of the Organisation, no consideration whatsoever was given to it. Neither did its needs and requirements figure in the grand designs for the several international institutions or agencies that were thereafter established. In fact, it never occurred to the 41 founder members that dependent territories in the present-day Third World would ever be free, or at least not so soon.

It can therefore be assumed that it was with shock and dismay that the rich countries began to view the first signs of change in the world order, in the middle and late fifties, as a number of dependent territories became free nations. The process of liberation continued unabated in the sixties and was intensified thereafter. By 1965 most colonial territories had become independent. By 1976 the Organisation, which began with 41 members, had grown to include more than 140. The organisation, at least on the surface, was no longer a rich man's club; it had become more of a poor man's club. But while the Organisation swelled numerically to put the 41 founder members into a minority, this did not affect, to any appreciable degree, the question of power and control within it. The industrialised nations, which have the power and control, still pursue policies and practices that were applicable to Europe in the 1940s, although the political, economic and social circumstances have changed. Thus the former relationships that existed between the metropolitan centres and their colonial dependencies still exist today between the industrialised countries and the so-called developing or Third-World countries. Moreover, it has become clear to most people that most of the international agencies of the United Nations, including those only marginally affiliated to it, are defenders of the international *status quo* and guardians of the vested interests of the industrialised world. Therefore they cannot be expected disinterestedly to carry out development programmes in the developing countries in a way that would disrupt the master–servant relationship existing today between industrialised and developing countries. If this is the case, then the question arises as to why these poor countries, most of which are in Africa, are eager to become members of every one of these agencies, even when the record of their performance has not been encouraging. What, basically, do they want from these institutions? Do they often achieve their objectives?

The answer to the first question may be obvious. One of the reasons, perhaps, is the legitimacy which it confers upon the young nation. Such legitimacy also guarantees her sovereignty as a nation, at least internationally. Thus membership is a ritual of acceptance into the world community of sovereignties. Legitimacy and guarantee of sovereignty is especially important to African countries, some of which are often bounded by hostile neighbours, either on account of ideological differences or territorial disagreements. In case of threat they can always cry to the world body for protection, even though such protection is not always effective. Moreover, in an interdependent world, it would be folly to live in isolation. For a lot of African countries, membership in the organisation is both for prestige and a form of advertisement. For a small country difficult to locate on a map, the opportunity to fly her flag over a building in New York and Geneva or for her president or prime minister to address the General Assembly, can be both materially rewarding and psychologically invigorating.

But while all these benefits are undeniable, often most African countries do not examine the disadvantages in order to balance them with the benefits, to see whether or not the financial and political price they pay for their membership is worthwhile. At face value, the financial price which a country pays is quite small. Even so, some of these countries are so small and poor that they cannot pay their annual dues. Moreover, the cost of maintaining a mission either in New York or in Geneva is often so high that such a country may find herself dipping into development funds. But the price such a small country pays should not be seen only in terms of money. As has happened in a number of cases, these countries have found themselves in a situation where they are able to maintain their membership or mission only through the 'generosity' of a former colonial patron, or some other rich country. Obviously, such 'generosity' has a price. In the distant past, when the United Nations was divided into only two main blocs, the West and the East, and the rest of the world had to fall in behind them on any General Assembly issue, a poor country which could not pay her dues was highly valued because the 'generous' patron could always count on her vote at crucial moments, even if the issue at stake was against the poor country's interests or the larger interests of the continent. While it would be argued that the present solidarity among the Third World countries has reduced the chances of such vote-selling, the financial constraints are nonetheless still there.

Moreover, it would also be argued that such financial constraints do not outweigh the benefits of membership, either to the individual country concerned or to the continent as a whole; that not only does the present numerical strength of the African countries at the UN derive from a collection of such mini-states, but also the individual poor state, through membership of the world body, enjoys the benefits that accrue from its several agencies. While the first argument, that is, that the continent derives power from having a large voting bloc, may be true, the second argument is difficult to accept. In fact, this argument goes to the root of what this chapter is primarily concerned with. For years it has generally been assumed by most African countries that the only way that they could develop is through close association with these development agencies. Therefore the tendency is for each country to become a member in every one of them, without first examining the purposes and objectives of these agencies, how they operate, and their relationships with the industrialised countries and their multinational companies and institutions. Most important, however, is whether or not, in fact, such an agency might be working against her national interests.

This brings us to the second question which we raised earlier: what do African countries really want from the international organisations? Obviously, they want financial aid and technical assistance. But beyond such generalities it is difficult to ascertain whether they have any clear notion of how best to achieve these aims. This may derive from the peculiarity of the institutions themselves. Nonetheless, the speed with which African nations rush to join them, and the enthusiasm with which they surrender aspects of their development planning to them, gives one cause to wonder if they are really aware of the complexities involved.

What, in fact, are the objectives of these institutions? John White, in 'International Agencies: the Case for Proliferation', in G. K. Helleiner (ed.), *A World Divided: the Less Developed Countries in the International Economy* (Cambridge: Cambridge University Press, 1976), pp. 275–93, indicates that the functions of international agencies could be grouped into six main categories:

(i) providing a framework for the resolution of conflicts between Member States;

(ii) promoting joint activities between Member States, which reap the advantages of scale, e.g. under complementary or production sharing agreements:

(iii) providing assistance in the mobilisation of resources;

(iv) providing advice in fields which require specialised technical skills;

(v) providing assistance in the recruitment of personnel or organisations to perform specified tasks, e.g. engineering contractors, or managing agents;

(vi) acting on Member countries' behalf in negotiations with external organisations, e.g. foreign private investors, or aid agencies. (p. 288)

While category (i) could be said to be almost totally innocuous (this function is useful especially to those countries in conflict), the same cannot be said for categories (ii) to (vi) if, as indicated earlier, some of these agencies position themselves as standard-bearers of the international economic *status quo* and in some cases represent the vested interests of the industrialised financial and economic institutions against whom the poor countries, whom they are supposed to be helping, are continuously struggling. Let us proceed to examine briefly each of these five categories.

Category (ii) undoubtedly confers many advantages on the

developing economies (that is, the raw material producers), the most important of which are the stabilisation of raw material prices and the availability of steady markets. Stabilisation of prices also has the advantage of allowing these producer countries to plan their development programmes far ahead. But why is it that, in spite of all these advantages, over the years these countries have experienced declined earnings from the same products, such as cocoa, even when the quantity has steadily increased? The most obvious answer would, of course, be that the manufactured products of the industrialised countries have increased over the same period, while the value of the raw material has been steady. What concerns us here, however, is: if stabilisation of prices is so advantageous, why is it that it is mainly commodity products of the developing countries that are included in these agreements? For example, why are not such products as soyabean and wheat—products almost wholly produced by the industrialised countries, but also in great demand in the developing countries—included? It would be argued that it is developing countries who most need such agreements, since their economic planning is based mainly on commodity products, which have a marginal effect on the budgets of industrialised nations. While this may be true, it nonetheless points out the inequality of such agreements. It is also argued by the producers that they are mainly for home consumption. To some extent this is true. But one needs to know to what extent the farmers (the producers), say, in the United States, are dependent on foreign markets to understand how flimsy, even ridiculous, such an argument about home consumption is.

While the commodities included in the agreements maintain steady prices therefore, commodities not included in the agreements have rocketed in price over the same period. Thus, on careful examination, this function of category (ii) is geared more to conflicts resolution (category (i)) than to genuinely desired mutual benefits as claimed by those who hold up these agreements as evidence of industrialised countries' magnanimity towards the developing world. But the success of such conflicts resolution, especially conflict between unequal parties, is not always easy to measure.

As for category (iii), this function is not regarded as a primary one by many international agencies; in fact, these agencies are 'more concerned with resources mobilisation for themselves, which they then transmit to their own clients at their own discretion'. White (op. cit.) has this to say about the World Bank, for instance:

> . . . the World Bank has never fulfilled what was originally seen as its principal role, namely the provision of an underwriting and guarantee facility which would enhance the *independent* [my italics] borrowing capacity of its clients. The most plausible explanation of this avoidance does not lie in any accident of the World Bank's evolution, but in the inherent conflict between helping its clients to borrow and borrowing for itself, since both increase its total exposure.

He goes on to argue that the claim that the World Bank has succeeded in increasing the total resources available to its developing member clients is unproven.

His arguments with regard to categories (iv) and (v) are also worth stating: 'In any field in which a country needs external advice, it is likely also to need advice on what sort of advice it needs'. He should have extended this, however, to include the fact that such a country would also need advice on what kind of advice has actually been given (invariably unsolicited) by an agency. The significance of this point is that it touches on the kinds of problems which are inherent to the function of 'advising' and it would not be an exaggeration to say that it is mainly here that most African countries exhibit their greatest ignorance and impotence. What are the problems actually involved? White notes two major problems:

> The need for advice about the kinds of advice needed means that extant agencies are continually drawn forward into pressing advice upon their clients. At the consultant level,

this may be regarded as a legitimate effort to get business. At the more pretentious level of international agencies, however, it shades into the dangerous area of policy prescription. National governments are more likely to want external advice in limited areas in which their policy objectives are already reasonably precise and clear than advice on what their policy objectives should be. The authors of heavy mission reports are usually satisfied if some, at least, of their recommendations are taken up on a selective basis, failing to recognise that this represents quite a different use of the report from the use implicit in the spirit in which it was written.

But there are other problems also:

(1) The advice given is often not by experts from the developing countries themselves, but by experts from the industrialised nations, who have very little knowledge of the environment and of the hidden internal problems of those developing countries.

(2) As a result of the above, the advice may in certain cases actually be wrong.

(3) The advice may not even be well understood by those who may put it into practice and even if it is understood, the fact that it does not always take local realities into consideration means that there would be a gulf between what the experts think and what the country perceives as its true problems; the result is therefore confusion and failure.

(4) The experts giving advice are not always impartial to the interests of their own countries, either as financial donors or as greatest contributors to the funds which may be used for the advising task; nor to the interests of their national companies which may want to be involved in the development projects for which they are providing the advice; nor, perhaps more importantly, to the interests of the sponsoring agency itself.

(5) The snowballing advice mechanism, that is, the chain process of the developing country seeking advice on the advice

wanted and advice given, may in the end prove extraordinarily expensive.

Category (v) is akin to category (iv), particularly since its principle is advisory rather than operational.

Of course, there is no easy way of resolving these problems, especially since the poor developing country needs expert advice, or technical assistance, either purely to implement her development programme or as conditions of financial aid. Yet, as for category (iv), it would be extremely useful if the developing country (a) knew the nature of such advice and then refused to subordinate her already formulated policy objectives to those of the advice-giving agency, and (b) more importantly, did not mistake advice for prescription. Furthermore, one seeks advice only on a subject about which one already has some concrete opinions or ideas, and not on a subject about which one is totally in the dark. In the latter case, such advice would be relatively useless, if not disastrous, since one does not know whether or not it is sound and therefore how to implement it. The advantage of knowing what one wants before seeking advice is that one can compare and select intelligently and the chances of mistaking advice for prescription are, at least, reduced.

As for category (v), one needs only to ask whether, in the light of imponderables involved, it might not be more useful for the developing country to hire outright certain people or organisations who could then be more directly accountable to the host country to do certain jobs, rather than rely solely on the international agency's technical assistance. Of course, this might be expensive, yet in the light of the possibility that an agency might impede or derail the programme, the course suggested above could in the long term prove more economical.

Category (vi), like the other functions mentioned, could be extremely useful to developing countries lacking expertise to negotiate trade agreements; but again it depends on the impartiality of such an agency and the level of its desire to actually see the developing country develop. In this respect,

one would have to say that UNCTAD, which offers negotiation services, and other regional agencies, has shown some
genuine desire to really help developing countries get a fair
deal. Yet it would be sad to note that UNCTAD, which offers
itself as representing developing countries' interests, and other
regional agencies which seem to be doing the most creditable
work and which seem to have the greatest will to help
developing countries, are, unfortunately, the least powerful
within the United Nations system. Why is this so?

It may seem cynical to suggest that it proves that the
industrialised countries who control the United Nations
system, particularly through their greater financial contributions, are not actually very interested in the developing
countries catching up with them. One indication of this is the
industrialised countries' attitudes in the so-called North-South
dialogue, which seeks to create a new international economic
order so that the developing countries can have a fairer
economic deal. While these industrialised countries piously
proclaim their desire to see a world more balanced than the
present one, it is clear that they are not yet interested in doing
those things which would bring their proclaimed desire to
fruition, such as the transfer of technology, better trading
arrangements and so forth. Furthermore, those who think this
assessment is premature need only take another, more concrete example: the World Bank and other financial institutions, as has been noted, tend to avoid industrial projects,
even the productive sector as a whole. Rather, they tend to be
interested in projects of limited social value, such as rural
clinics, schools, rural lighting, and population control. The
argument for this is that industry belongs to the private sector.
At first, such an argument may seem harmless; but on closer
examination, it appears rather cynical, since the so-called
industry is often not in the control of the developing country
herself, but in the hands of companies and multinational
institutions of the industrialised countries who own or control
the financial institutions themselves.

There are other ways in which international institutions,

while appearing virtuous in their dealings, actually impede the development process in the developing countries. For example, these international institutions, because they often press their advice and policy objectives on the recipient developing country, invariably preclude policy alternatives that may be more useful to the developing country. Also, specialised agencies, because they are often promoting their own areas of interest or responsibility, place emphasis on one sector or another of the economy, almost to the total neglect of other areas which may have greater potential. Thus, a country like Senegal, as Samir Amin has noted in our earlier chapters, is almost perpetually consigned to groundnut growing, when she could, in fact, have done better by developing other agricultural products. Here is his observation:

> If the thousands of millions invested in infrastructure for the groundnut basin had been invested instead to provide a proper irrigation infrastructure in these three areas (the River Valley, the Niayes, and Lower and Central Casamance), intensive cultivation and modern forms of agriculture could have been developed here on a large scale: for high yields of rice and sugar cane, and high quality produce (early vegetables and fruits, oil-palms in Casamance). The main potential of the present groundnut basin, too, is not in fact groundnuts, but intensive modern livestock rearing and the cultivation of fodder such as beetroot in rotation with millet and groundnuts . . . A further possibility is deep-sea fishing, for which conditions on the coasts of Senegal are exceptionally favourable. Technical problems certainly exist; but so far they have not been seriously studied, even though it is almost certain that they can be solved.

The Institute for Research into Oil and Oil-producing Substances (IRHO) is, of course, not interested in anything but groundnuts because that is what Senegal is told she is good at, and moreover it is what France perhaps needs most.

But perhaps the greatest problem with all international

institutions is that there is no way of assessing their performance in each developing country. To a certain degree, of course, this is not true; methods of measuring success or failure could be found. It is merely that these organisations resist such evaluation, because, as White (op. cit.) has noted in his article:

> The organs and agencies of the UN are portrayed as the intermediate embodiment of an ultimate ideal of global harmony, or even of world government. Their claim on their members' resources is based, not on assessment of their record, but on their inherent virtue as the earthly representative of the ideal, and their opponents are manoeuvred into the position of seeming to be on the side of sin.

To justify and maintain this posture of being the embodiment of the ideal and of virtue; they 'tend to avoid enterprises in which profitability is a criterion, precisely because it would lead to a very clear test of their performance'. The claim to universality and to a universal ideal and virtue means that they are accountable to no-one but themselves. Hence, when the programmes on which they give advice or policy objectives founder, the blame is not put at their door but at that of the poor recipient developing country.

Now, let us look at another side of international organs of the UN. As I have earlier indicated, the inequality that exists between rich and poor countries also exists in these institutions. This is so for three main reasons:

(1) As founder-members, the industrialised countries control the institutions and the institutions, from the beginning, were geared to their interests.

(2) Because they are wealthy, the industrialised countries contribute the bulk of operational funds, and in spite of any virtuous views to the contrary, he who pays the piper calls the tune.

(3) These institutions are mainly specialised organs and as such they require expert skills to which the industrialised countries lay a monopoly claim. Thus they are dominated by

experts from the industrialised countries.

In the last few years some of these institutions have been going through some upheavals. Some of the developing countries say they only want to claim their just say in the running of the institutions. They say that if the ideal of the institutions is democracy, they want to see that the majority will prevail. The industrialised countries, on the other hand, say that the developing countries are misusing their majority votes to politicise the organisations which hitherto, they argue, had been bastions of goodwill and neutrality. Furthermore, it is contended that the tenets of democracy cannot always depend only on a majority basis, particularly if it is the minority that pays the bills. The difficulty with these arguments is that they are both right. A more basic problem with the industrialised world's argument, however, is that it is often raised to a level of virtue. Worse still, often they judge the standards of democracy in these organisations, not by standards set in the organisations' charter or constitutions, but by standards supposedly inherent, in their individual countries. Hence, not too long ago the United States Congress passed a resolution praising the level of democracy in the American Federation of Labor-Committee of Industrial Organisation (AFL-CIO) and urging all international organisations, particularly the International Labour Organisation, to emulate it. Thus one is led to think that the current problems with the ILO derive largely from the fact that the United States does not think that the Organisation has heeded her congressional resolution. And as a result they have pulled out of the Organisation. But this, in itself, is a prime example of how big-power politics work within the UN organisation—the forcing of one power's will on the rest of the members—and of how democracy is not supposed to work.

As part of the virtuous stand of the United States, the *New York Times* wrote an editorial in the *International Herald Tribune* (15 August, 1977), indicating how the Organisation would be reduced to impotence if the United States were to withdraw. It is true that the United States pays 25 per cent of the ILO budget and, as a result, the Organisation could actually be forced to curtail 'useful and necessary work'. But it would also be useful to look at the situation more objectively to see whether this large contribution is actually merely for charity.

First of all, it should be noted that about 65–70 per cent of the ILO budget goes on salaries and field trips. That means that only about 25–35 per cent of the budget is actually devoted to 'useful and necessary work', that is, to programmes, most of which, admittedly, are in the developing countries.

But the fact that 25–35 per cent of the funds are spent in developing countries could be misleading. For example, in 1976, out of a $5 million budget for programmes in the developing countries, $3 million went for expert services—obviously nearly all these experts are from the industrialised countries; which means that, in actual fact, only $2 million went into the programmes. Now, let us look at the employee statistics. Of the 2,000 employees of the ILO, only 45 are Africans. Three-quarters of the total employees of the Organisation are either French or British. If the United States does not figure prominently here, it is not because she is not adequately represented: she is dominant in the top segments of the various departments. Moreover, she has more than her fair share of representation in those organisations based in New York. American generosity in Geneva is towards her European allies, France and Britain, while in New York these allies show similar generosity towards her. In any case, it is to be noted that the experts who consumed 60 per cent of the budget last year for development programmes in the developing countries also come from these three countries.

The above should be seen in the light of the fact that in the entire ILO, there are only five Africans who could be said to be in top positions. Of these five, only one is in a decision-making position and, that is in the academic area. The other four are in departmental-level decision-making positions and are subordinate to heads from the industrialised countries, mainly France, Britain and the United States. The key decision-making positions – that is, for budget and programming—are also held by members of these three countries.

If an example is made of the ILO, it is not because it is the only organisation guilty of this hypocrisy. The same pattern of organisational structure prevails in nearly all the international organisations. Not long ago, the director of the Food and Agriculture Organization (FAO) made the same observation that about 75 per cent of that Organization's budget goes on administrative services. And again, the employment structure is the same as for the ILO. The same applies to the United Nations Development Programme (UNDP). It is true the United States pays about 80 per cent of the budget, but she then insists that the agency's experts must be recruited from the US. Of course, this is fair enough, if we accept that he who pays the piper calls the tune. That this precept is insisted upon by the industrialised countries was indicated a few years ago when there was an international outcry against the practices of the multinational companies. The demand by the Third-World countries that their experts also be involved in the ILO investigation of the companies was rejected by the key decision-making officials of the Organisation. Instead, experts were brought in from the United States, which, to many developing countries, was like asking a criminal to investigate himself. Now, we can only imagine the result if the Third-World countries were to have equal power with the US, France and Britain, and had participated in the investigation of these multinationals. Needless to say, the opportunity for the industrialised countries to investigate themselves without any intrusion from the Third World countries is one of the benefits enjoyed by the Western members of these organisations.

But there are other more pernicious ways in which the industrialised states reap disproportionate benefits from these organisations, while the developing countries are continuously on the losing end. One is that the developing countries are continuously exposed to the invasion of international civil servants under the pretext of international cooperation. Thus, while these developing countries know nothing about the national economies of the industrialised world, the experts from the latter know every secret of the former. And one does not need to understand the relationship between these international civil servants, that is, the experts, and their governments, corporations, and companies, and their national labour unions, to understand what kind of secret information traffic flows from the developing countries into the industrialised world, which the former is not aware of. Hence any question of competitiveness in the market-place between the industrialised and the developing countries is really pure nonsense.

Now, after the preceding analysis, it seems reasonably obvious to say that when everything is added up— employment, control over decisions about development programmes, fees paid to experts, the possibility of these experts working for the interests of their own countries and not as neutral servants—the industrialised countries reap nearly all the benefits to be gained from international organisations. Not only that, but as the industrialised world gains, so the developing world loses.

But the wonder is not that this is the case, but rather, why most African countries still join these organisations if they invariably lose out ultimately. Is it that they believe that what they gain outweighs their loss? Or is it because they are not actually aware of their own losses? That the latter might be the case is indicated by the fact that they subscribe even to such little-understood organisations as WIPO, the so-called World Intellectual Property Organisation, and more curiously that they should have signed its convention on copyright.

Had the African nations understood the preceding considerations and taken them into account, and had they recognised their thirst for knowledge and shown a desire to spread that knowledge cheaply to their peoples, then obviously they would not have subscribed to such a convention. In fact the course of action advocated here becomes more useful, especially since publishing in most African countries is state-owned, and it would be easier for such publishing houses to lay hands on a badly-needed foreign book and publish it cheaply for her schools and intellectually starving public. If this course of action seems peculiar or even illegal, then perhaps one should remember that a little breaking of the international rules of protocol is sometimes useful.

From the preceding analysis, it is clear that a number of reasons are responsible for the African countries' rush to join these international institutions. The first is the lack of understanding of the actual workings of the institutions, that is, a lack of understanding of their effects on developing countries. This lack of understanding could, on the one hand, be attributed to the failure of the institutions themselves to make such relevant information available. But most importantly, it is the failure of the countries themselves to *seek* such information. The lack of desire to seek information may also derive from the countries not knowing what they actually want or expect from these institutions.

So what can Nigeria do? There are certain actions she can take to lead the way for other African countries, especially since she has the financial and intellectual resources:

(1) The first step should be for her to set up a separate, independent institute whose primary concern should be to monitor all specialised international agencies. The institute should be able to compile information on these agencies and to make such information available to other African countries who may need it, either before or after joining such an agency.

(2) Such an institute could also act as a 'think-tank' to advise, upon request, other African states who may seek any agency's advice or technical assistance.

If the above suggestion is considered and taken seriously, it could become one of the best forms of economic and technical aid Nigeria could possibly provide for other African countries.

Index

Abbreviations and acronyms are grouped together at the beginning of the initial letter